American History Made Easy

For ESL Learners

Kathleen Gripman

For more information and further discussion, visit

SpeakLearnSucceed.com

Cover art and design by
Rick Nease
www.RickNeaseArt.com

Published by Step Up Success
Publishing services provided by Front Edge Publishing, LLC

For information about customized editions, bulk purchases or permissions, contact Front Edge Publishing, LLC at info@FrontEdgePublishing.com

Contents

Coming to America
1492-1776

Desire for Self-Government

The English were the first northern Europeans to **settle** in America in the 100 years after Columbus discovered the "New World" in 1492. England saw that Spain was **claiming** a lot of the land and many Spaniards were becoming wealthy in the New World. Some English people thought they could find treasures in the new land too, so they asked Queen Elizabeth for permission to go to America.

Sir Walter Raleigh **founded** a colony (an area controlled by another country) in North America in 1585. His ships sailed to an island near what is now North Carolina. The colonists looked for gold, but never found any. They had to ask the American Indians (also called "Native Americans") for food, because they were too interested in looking for gold to grow food.

The English thought that their way of life was better than the Indians' way, and that made the Indians angry. The Indians gave them a little food, but it wasn't enough, so the English went home. Then, Raleigh brought more **settlers** to America and, this time, they stayed. In 1587, Virginia Dare was the first English baby born in the New World. When another ship arrived in 1591, all of the settlers were gone. The only **clue** about what had happened to them was an Indian word **carved** on a doorpost. The settlers were never seen again, so it is called "The Lost Colony."

In 1607, Jamestown, the first important English settlement in America was founded in what is now Virginia. Jamestown succeeded, but had many hard times. The village was near a swamp that was full of disease-carrying mosquitoes. Colony leader John Smith helped the Colonists, but 68 of the 100 settlers died of illness or starvation before their first Christmas. They foolishly did not plant corn until Smith made them stop looking for gold.

Powhatan, a powerful Indian chief, gave the settlers food in exchange for help fighting his Indian enemies. Over time, the English and the Indians began to fight each other, because the English cheated the Indians and were cruel to them. The Indians captured John Smith. Powhatan planned to free him, but a **legend** (a historical story that is probably not true) claimed that Powhatan's daughter, Pocahontas, was in love with John Smith and saved him. (Actually, Pocahontas married another Englishman and went to England.)

In 1620, the **Pilgrims** sailed a ship called the *Mayflower* to a place near where Boston, Massachusetts is today. The Pilgrims were very religious. They left England because they were not allowed to **worship** the way they wanted. Friendly Indians saved the Pilgrims from starving during their first winter in the New World. The next fall, the Pilgrims thanked God for the food that the Indians had shown them how to plant and hunt. They celebrated with a special feast they called "Thanksgiving" that is still celebrated today.

In Jamestown and Boston, the Colonists wrote a plan to govern themselves, to create their own laws. It became an American custom to use

The First Thanksgiving

a written document as an **authority** on governing, rather than a king or queen.

Other English settlers followed the Pilgrims to America. The Quakers also left England to escape religious **persecution**. They believed in a peaceful life and were against any type of violence. One of the most famous Quakers was William Penn, who helped found the Pennsylvania Colony. Another group, the Puritans, started the Massachusetts Bay Colony and it grew very large. They believed God had chosen them to lead everyone. They were very strict and they punished anyone who disagreed with them by making them leave the Colony. The Puritans were very educated, so as the **Colonies** grew, they became the upper class in Boston.

As the Colonists traded more and more with other countries, the merchant class became very **wealthy**. Money and property decided a person's position in American society, rather than **ancestry**.

Settlers kept coming from England and Europe, including people from different religious groups, people who were friends of the English king, and people who came with businesses. Eventually, the settlers founded 13 Colonies in eastern America.

A large group of people who came to America did not want to come. They liked their lives in Africa, where they had their own villages, families, fields, animals, religion and arts. They were kidnapped and forced to come as slaves (people owned by other people). They were chained, and many died on the terrible two-month voyage across the Atlantic Ocean. Most African slaves in America were sold to people who owned large tobacco, rice and cotton farms in the South, called **plantations**. Most slaves were forced to work very hard in the fields and were treated cruelly.

More Colonists arrived, and they wanted more land. They moved farther and farther west for more than 100 years. They fought the French and Indians for the land, but King George III of England said the Indians should have it. The King also made many other laws that the Colonists didn't like, and his taxes made everything expensive. The disagreement over the English laws in America made everyone angry and nervous. After British soldiers fired guns into a Boston crowd and killed or wounded about a dozen Colonists, news of this "Boston **Massacre**" made Americans furious. The King also said the Colonists had to pay a tax on the tea that came on the ships. An angry group in Boston dressed up as Mohawk Indians and dumped all the tea off the ship and into the water in protest. This was called the "Boston Tea Party." The Colonists, who had no control over laws and taxes in America, complained that there should be "no taxation without representation!"

Many Colonists, especially in Virginia and Massachusetts, agreed that America should be free from the king. In Massachusetts, they formed bands of men called "minutemen." They could be ready to fight British soldiers very quickly (in a minute).

The Colonists were afraid the British would take their weapons away. One Colonist, a **patriot** named Paul Revere, arranged a signal. The signal was: "One if by land, two if by sea." One lantern would warn Revere that the British soldiers were marching from Boston to Concord. Two lanterns said the British were coming by boat. After he got the signal, Revere was to ride his horse through Concord to warn the people there.

Another leader of the movement to break away from English control was Benjamin Franklin. He was well-known as a publisher, politician, ambassador, scientist and inventor. He established the first fire department, and invented a **furnace** to keep buildings safe and warm. It was called the Franklin stove. He grew up poor, but worked hard and became successful in the new country. His picture is on the $100 bill. He was very helpful in keeping everyone focused on creating a new system of government and telling everyone about the benefits of this new country.

Paul Revere and the Old North Church

Fighting For Self-Government

On April 18, 1775, Paul Revere saw two lanterns in the window of the church tower. He knew that meant that the British were coming by sea. Legend says he jumped on his horse and galloped through the night shouting, "The **redcoats** are coming!" Actually, Revere and two other men rode from Boston to warn patriots in Concord and Lexington that the British army was marching toward them. Revere avoided the redcoats and reached Lexington, but was captured before he could get to Concord. One of the other riders got through to Concord.

Thanks to the warnings, the minutemen were prepared for the battles of Lexington and Concord, which happened the next day. These were the first battles of the American Revolution. Another **fierce** battle was fought in June 1775 at Bunker Hill, near Boston, Massachusetts. British troops eventually forced the Americans to **retreat**, but more than 1,000 British soldiers were killed or wounded.

Delegates from all 13 of the American Colonies met in Philadelphia. The meeting, called the Second Continental **Congress**, began on May 10, 1775, and **lasted** more than a year. Benjamin Franklin was a delegate. The delegates finally approved Thomas Jefferson's *Declaration of Independence* on July 4, 1776 (see Appendix B). The *Declaration of Independence*, which was written by Jefferson, said that Americans would rule themselves. Jefferson believed that government is a contract between the government and the people. If the government did not live up to the contract, the people had the **right** to change the government or create a new one.

Then, the new country had to support its declaration by fighting England's better-trained and better-**armed** military. British soldiers were used to taking orders and fighting under generals. Congress asked Americans to join the army to fight for their independence. At this time, Americans only had small, local military units called **militia**. The militias were eager, but not disciplined. Americans were independent people who sometimes argued not only about who their leaders should be, but also about obeying orders. If they didn't like the leader or the orders, they just went home. Americans had no national plan, or money, to give the soldiers uniforms, weapons or even food.

Most Americans didn't even consider themselves "Americans" yet. They called themselves **citizens** of individual states. It was more typical for a person to say, "I'm a Virginian," or "I'm from Massachusetts," than to say "I'm an American." Not everyone even agreed that America should be free from

England. Some Colonists called Loyalists (or Tories) wanted the former Colonies to remain British.

General George Washington was the commander-in-chief of the Continental (American) Army. He didn't have enough food, weapons or soldiers. The men he did have were not trained soldiers, but the Americans still knew things that the British did not know. They knew the wilderness, where they could use the trees as **shields** against British guns.

The Americans also had another advantage. The British were separated from England by the Atlantic Ocean. It took months to sail from England to America, and even longer to return. The British soldiers had to get almost all of their replacements and supplies from England.

Another American advantage was that American soldiers were inspired by the ideas of liberty and independence. They wanted to fight for themselves. They didn't have uniforms, enough food or much ammunition, but they wanted to make their dream come true.

By the time America **declared** independence, Washington had gathered about 20,000 American soldiers. The early months of the Revolution were hard. Many Americans were killed, wounded or captured in terrible battles

Minutemen Attacking British Troops

in New York. Some American soldiers just went home. By December 1776, Washington only had 3,000 men left. Weary and **discouraged**, they escaped to New Jersey. The situation was so bad that some Americans began to wonder if it had been a mistake to break away from Britain. Some remained hopeful.

Thomas Paine, the author of *Common Sense* (a **pamphlet** that inspired many Americans to break from Britain) wrote, "These are the times that try men's souls." (By "try," Paine meant "test.") These discouraging days would test whether Americans had enough determination to continue fighting. Paine continued, "The summer soldier and the sunshine patriot will, in this crisis, shrink from the service of his country, but he that stands it now deserves the love and thanks of man and woman." This pamphlet was widely read by the American colonists.

Washington and his remaining troops needed a victory. They got it in a daring surprise attack on Christmas night, December 25, 1776. About 1,000 Hessian troops (German soldiers who worked for the British)

General George Washington and the American Troops

The 13 Original Colonies

were camped in Trenton, New Jersey. The Americans secretly crossed the icy Delaware River in small boats that night, and caught the Hessians by surprise. Over 600 Hessian troops were killed or captured. This victory and others in the next few months encouraged the Americans, but there were still many challenges ahead. Washington still needed more soldiers and more money. Congress offered $20 and 100 acres of free land in the West to each new **recruit** to help increase the size of the army. Finally, Washington had 9,000 men by the spring. Many wealthy colonists and European countries lent money to the colonies to help support the war.

The battle at Saratoga, New York turned the war to the Americans' advantage. The British sent General John Burgoyne and thousands of troops from Canada. They were ordered to isolate the New England states (over half of the former Colonies) from the rest.

Many American soldiers were dressed in rags and half starved, but General Burgoyne had wagons filled with his **belongings**, including cases of champagne and even silver dishes. The march south took Burgoyne and his troops months longer than they expected. The British ran out of food. Supplies and **reinforcements** never arrived from across the ocean. Burgoyne's troops grew weaker, but the Continental Army grew stronger as more Americans joined the cause. Americans defeated Burgoyne at Saratoga in October 1777. The **proud** British general had to **surrender** almost 6,000 men to the **rebels**.

In 1777, Congress chose the American flag, with 13 red and white alternating stripes, and 13 white stars on a field of blue. It represented the 13 Colonies that were fighting for their independence.

The victory at Saratoga brought the Americans a strong **ally**: France. The French had fought the English on and off for centuries, so they wanted to see the British army defeated. At first, the French still thought the rebels could never defeat the mighty British, so they did not tell anyone they supported the Americans. Instead, early in the Revolution, they secretly sent supplies, especially gunpowder. Then, the victory at Saratoga convinced French King Louis XVI that the Americans might actually win. So, he shipped weapons, ammunition and, eventually, troops to America.

Individual officers from other European nations also joined the American **struggle** for independence. General Bernardo de Galvez led Spanish troops against the British in what is now Florida. A Polish engineer, Thaddeus Kosciuszko, gave Americans expert advice on how to plan battles and build forts. A Prussian general, Friedrich Wilhelm von Steuben, taught Washington's troops professional military techniques.

One young Frenchman was so eager to join the war that he disobeyed a direct order from the French king. The Marquis de Lafayette, an ambitious young French nobleman, wanted the glory of becoming a commanding officer in the American Revolution. The French were not openly supporting America yet, so Louis XVI ordered Lafayette to stay in France, but Lafayette disobeyed. He was caught, but escaped, and sailed to America.

In the summer of 1777, when he was only 19, he met Washington in Philadelphia. Washington gave Lafayette command of a division of soldiers. He later became a general in the Continental Army and fought for four years. When the war ended, he returned to France but kept his strong attachment to America. The king forgave him for disobeying.

Many Americans celebrated the victory at Saratoga and the French **alliance**. At this point in the war, Washington and his troops were sick, freezing and starving at Valley Forge in the bitter winter of 1777, while the British stayed warm and comfortable. Valley Forge was the low point of the Revolution. Many men died and many others went home.

One of Washington's other generals, General Benedict Arnold, was a successful American military leader, even a hero. For most of the war, he thought he should be promoted, but he wasn't. In 1780, Americans captured a British soldier. In his boot they found a letter that said Arnold would, in exchange for money, give the American fort at West Point, New York, to the British. Arnold escaped to England, but his **treason** upset people so much that an American **traitor** is still called a "Benedict Arnold."

British General Lord Charles Cornwallis believed that England could only win the war if it captured Virginia. Yorktown, Virginia, near the site of the early Jamestown settlement, is located on a **peninsula**. When Cornwallis put his troops there, Washington and his troops **cornered** them. Thousands of French soldiers, some under the command of Lafayette, joined Washington to surround the British on land, while the French Navy sailed into Chesapeake Bay and cut off a British escape by sea. Both American and French guns **pounded** Cornwallis' troops and he was finally forced to surrender in October of 1781.

When news of the defeat reached Britain, one leader in **Parliament** declared the war over. Both sides fought a few more battles, but the American victory at Yorktown marked the end of the Revolutionary War.

Cornwallis recognized the daring and bravery of the Americans, and ordered the British band to play "The World Turned Upside Down," because no one was supposed to be able to defeat the British. Some legends say that Lafayette responded by ordering the band to play "Yankee Doodle." Before the Revolution, Americans might have gotten angry if the British had called them Yankee doodles, because Yankee was an **offensive** name for a New Englander, and doodle meant foolish person. However, during the Revolution, American soldiers started to consider the song a statement of pride. If you read all of the verses, you can see how "Yankee Doodle" became a symbol of the courageous, determined and independent American spirit.

Yankee Doodle

Yankee Doodle went to town
A-riding on a pony
Stuck a feather in his hat
And called it macaroni.

Yankee Doodle, keep it up
Yankee Doodle dandy
Mind the music and the step
And with the girls be handy.

Father and I went down to camp
Along with Captain Gooding
And there we saw the men and boys
As thick as hasty pudding.

Yankee Doodle, keep it up
Yankee Doodle dandy
Mind the music and the step
And with the girls be handy.

There was Captain Washington
Upon a slapping stallion
A-giving orders to his men
I guess there was a million.

Yankee Doodle, keep it up
Yankee Doodle dandy
Mind the music and the step
And with the girls be handy.

Becoming the United States 1787-1850

Trials of Self-Government

In 1783, a peace **treaty** with Britain gave America all of the land from the East Coast to the Mississippi River. Now the United States had to create its own government. Americans believed in the same liberties as the English. They fought for freedom only because the British wouldn't give those rights and liberties to the Colonists.

The leaders of the former Colonies also considered the histories of Greece and Rome, and the rights in the **Magna Carta**. They wanted the people to be represented in government. They had read the works of great philosophers who believed in "natural rights." They agreed that it is obvious, reasonable and natural that people have certain rights. So, in the Declaration of Independence, Thomas Jefferson listed three **inalienable** natural rights: "life, liberty and the pursuit of happiness." It also states: "We hold these truths to be self-evident, that all men are created equal." A self-evident truth is a clear and obvious truth.

Some people throughout history and around the world disagreed with this idea of natural rights (the **caste system** in India and ancient Rome, **feudalism** in England and **slavery** in America). When it said, "all men are created equal," the Declaration of Independence said that no one—not a king, pope, lord or emperor—can take away natural rights.

The idea of natural rights was not new, but the idea that government should respect and protect people's natural rights was revolutionary. If

IN CONGRESS, July 4, 1776

The Unanimous Declaration *of the thirteen united* States of America

When in the Course of human events, it becomes necessary for one people to dissolve the political bands which have connected them with another, and to assume among the powers of the earth, the separate and equal station to which the Laws of Nature and of Nature's God entitle them, a decent respect to the opinions of mankind requires that they should declare the causes which impel them to the separation.

We hold these truths to be self-evident, that all men are created equal, that they are endowed by their Creator with certain unalienable Rights, that among these are Life, Liberty and the pursuit of Happiness.--That to secure these rights, Governments are instituted among Men, deriving their just powers from the consent of the governed, --That whenever any Form of Government becomes destructive of these ends, it is the Right of the People to alter or to abolish it, and to institute new Government, laying its foundation on such principles and organizing its powers in such form, as to them shall seem most likely to effect their Safety and Happiness. Prudence, indeed, will dictate that Governments long established should not be changed for light and transient causes; and accordingly all experience hath shewn, that mankind are more disposed to suffer, while evils are sufferable, than to right themselves by abolishing the forms to which they are accustomed. But when a long train of abuses and usurpations, pursuing invariably the same Object evinces a design to reduce them under absolute Despotism, it is their right, it is their duty, to throw off such Government, and to provide new Guards for their future security.--Such has been the patient sufferance of these Colonies; and such is now the necessity which constrains them to alter their former Systems of Government. The history of the present King of Great Britain is a history of repeated injuries and usurpations, all having in direct object the establishment of an absolute Tyranny over these States. To prove this, let Facts be submitted to a candid world

Declaration of Independence

the U.S. government tries to take away your rights, the *Declaration of Independence* tells people they can—must—change the government.

So the Americans threw off the government of Britain.

Now what kind of government could they create to protect their natural rights? A Roman Senate? An English Parliament? There was no perfect model to imitate. American leaders had high ideals, like "life, liberty and the pursuit of happiness," but they didn't agree on what those ideals meant. Did liberty **grant** the freedom to do anything, even if it offended or hurt people? It was difficult to decide what was allowed and what was not. The new government had to be very careful when it defined liberty.

There were some big contradictions (opposite ideas or statements) in America. The *Declaration of Independence* said, "All men are created equal," even though some people were rich and others were poor. Governments had always represented wealthy people more than people who weren't rich. There was also an even bigger contradiction: some Americans owned slaves. How could people believe in liberty and slavery at the same time?

This contradiction was part of Western civilization for almost 2,000 years, from ancient Greeks, who believed in **democracy**, to 19th-**century** Britons and Americans. Every race has committed this terrible injustice of treating people as property. Slavery was even permitted by the great religions such as Christianity, Hinduism, Islam and Judaism. A tradition of injustice doesn't make it right. Americans still struggle with contradictions. It's a constant challenge to live up to the American ideals of the inalienable right to "life, liberty and the pursuit of happiness."

Today, each American state has its own government, but the federal government unites the states as one nation. The federal government is located in the national capital, Washington, D.C. The city is not located in a state, but in the District of Columbia, so no individual state is more special than any other. The president of the United States leads the federal government. Governors lead each of the 50 states. How did the U.S. get to this system of government?

When this first group of **representatives** designed the new government, all 13 states had their own cities, boundaries, and **legislatures**, as well as their own constitutions and currency. They had to decide how all of the states would work together.

America's new government wouldn't be like England's. That strong centralized government had tried to take away the natural rights of Americans. The new Americans agreed that the federal government should not have too much power. So, the Continental Congress created the *Articles of* **Confederation** in 1777. The agreement said:

- State governments could rule themselves.

- The federal government would have little power.

- Each state had only one vote in the **federal** government, no matter how big the state was, or how many people lived there.

- All decisions had to be unanimously approved before any action could take place.

It was very difficult to get all 13 states to agree completely on every decision.

The new government was less than 5 years old when many people started wanting a better one. The new nation was struggling, and some people **blamed** the weak central government. Merchants were ruined because Britain wouldn't sign separate trade agreements with each of the 13 states, and Congress didn't have the power to interfere. Some people worried that the British soldiers who were still in Canada would try to turn the United States back into colonies. If this happened, Congress could declare war, but it had no power to make the states supply soldiers, or tax the states to pay for the war. It became obvious that America needed to be able to speak and act as one nation. The *Articles of Confederation* had to be changed.

State delegates traveled to Philadelphia in 1787 for a Constitutional **Convention.** The delegates came from every state except Rhode Island, which refused to participate. The delegates finally approved the document that is still the highest law of the land—the **Constitution** *of the United States* (see Appendix C).

When the convention began, however, many of the 55 delegates just wanted to improve the existing *Articles of Confederation.* If they had known that they would be writing a national constitution, many of them, who were more **loyal** to their states than to the **fledgling** nation, might not have attended.

Many of the lawyers, merchants and farmers had fought in the Revolution. Some of them, George Washington, James Madison, Alexander Hamilton and Benjamin Franklin, were called the "Founding Fathers" because they played such important roles in creating and shaping the new nation.

James Madison, now known as the "Father of the Constitution," arrived early. He knew that the country couldn't just **tinker** with the *Articles of Confederation.* He wrote a plan for a strong centralized federal government. He proposed a government with three parts, or branches—**executive**, **legislative** and **judicial**.

Three Branches of Government

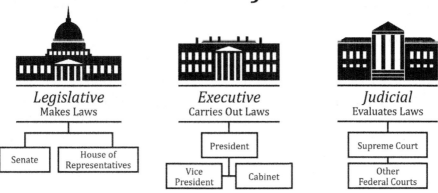

Legislative
Makes Laws

Senate | House of Representatives

Executive
Carries Out Laws

President

Vice President | Cabinet

Judicial
Evaluates Laws

Supreme Court

Other Federal Courts

1. The executive branch would run the government. Executives are the leaders or managers; the people in charge.
2. The legislative branch would write the laws. Madison proposed two parts to the legislative branch, or Congress:
   a. The **House of Representatives**, with representatives **elected** by the American people.
   b. The **Senate**, a smaller body of lawmakers chosen by members of the House of Representatives (like the ancient Romans).
3. The judicial branch would run the federal courts. They would be **headed** by a **Supreme** Court, which would **interpret** the laws of the land.

Each branch would have certain powers, and a system of checks and balances would be created to keep any single branch of government from becoming too powerful. Any branch had the power to **check**, or stop, another branch if it tried to do something not allowed in the Constitution. That would keep the power balanced among the three branches.

If, for example, Congress passes a law that the president doesn't like, he can **veto** it, or refuse to approve it. However, Congress can **override** the president's veto, if two-thirds of Congress vote for the law.

At first, the Supreme Court had six judges. Now it has nine judges, called justices. The leader is the chief justice. Justices are **appointed** by the president, but must be approved by the Senate. In 1981, Sandra Day O'Connor became the first woman justice.

The delegates argued about Madison's plan all through the hot summer of 1787. One argument was about the executive branch. Some delegates didn't believe the country needed a president. Experience with King George III made delegates **distrustful** of a single, powerful leader. Other delegates said America was weak because it didn't have a strong leader to deal with the leaders of other countries or to command the military.

In the end, the delegates agreed to have a president, but they limited the president's power. Unlike a king, a president wouldn't rule for life. He had to run for election every four years. The legislative branch could remove a bad president from office. The delegates also agreed that the president should have a vice president, who could replace the president, if necessary.

Congress was given the power to raise money directly from citizens, with taxes. Since Congress would consist of representatives elected by the American people, this would be taxation *with* representation. Members of the three branches would be paid from the national **treasury**, not by the states. The nation, however, needed money. Before the Constitutional Convention, people only paid taxes to the states, but a national army and

How Are Laws Passed?

A law begins with a proposal called a bill. Most bills can start in either the House of Representatives or the Senate. Before a bill becomes a law, both branches of Congress must vote for it.

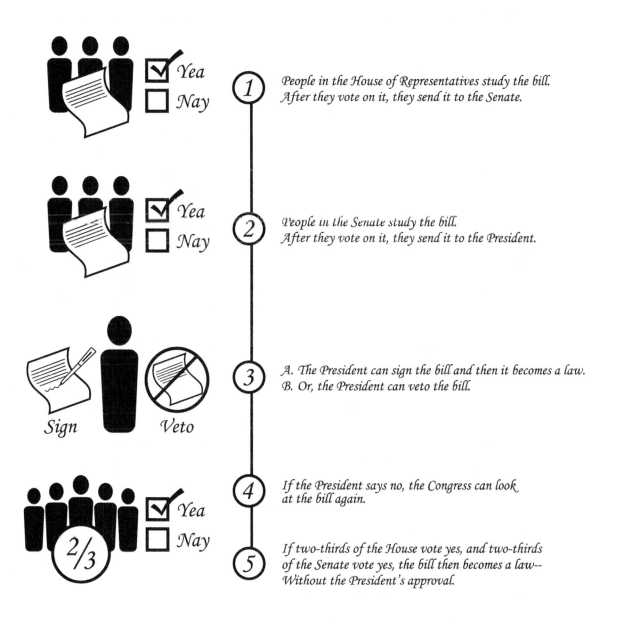

Yea ☑ / Nay ☐

1. *People in the House of Representatives study the bill. After they vote on it, they send it to the Senate.*

2. *People in the Senate study the bill. After they vote on it, they send it to the President.*

Sign — Veto

3. *A. The President can sign the bill and then it becomes a law.*
   B. Or, the President can veto the bill.

4. *If the President says no, the Congress can look at the bill again.*

5. *If two-thirds of the House vote yes, and two-thirds of the Senate vote yes, the bill then becomes a law-- Without the President's approval.*

navy need equipment, weapons and money to pay the soldiers and sailors. Today, Americans still pay taxes to the federal government for services like a strong military, highways and bridges, medical care for older people, missions to outer space and loans to help people pay for college.

The delegates gave Congress the power to tax, but couldn't agree on how many representatives each state should have in Congress. In Madison's plan, the states with more people would have more representatives. That gave the bigger states more power in running (managing) the government. The smaller states, with fewer people, wanted every state to have the same number of representatives in Congress. The big states said a small state should not have as much power as a big state. Delegates from the small states threatened to leave.

The delegates finally compromised. The size of the House of Representatives would be based on the population of each state. The bigger states would have more representatives than the smaller states, but every state would have the same number of senators. Both the House of Representatives and the Senate would have to agree on every law they passed, but the votes did not have to be unanimous. That's still the way it is today. One thing has changed: Senators have been elected directly by the people—not the State Senate—since 1913.

The Constitutional Convention approved the *Constitution* in September 1787. The new system turned a loose confederation of states into "a more perfect union." The new government was not perfect, but it was fairer than any previous system.

One of the most important features of the *Constitution* is that it makes both the national government and the states responsible for running the country. This division of power between the state and the national government is called the federal system.

Congressional powers are listed in the *Constitution*. The states keep all of the powers that are not specifically assigned to Congress (see Section 8 of the *Constitution*, Congress's powers in Appendix C). The *Constitution* is the book of rules for the government, which has three jobs:

1. Make the rules (laws) for the United States.
2. Run the country:
   a. Command the military.
   b. Make sure the people obey the law.
   c. Manage tax money.
   d. Make agreements with other countries.
   e. Help build roads and bridges (added later).
   f. Keep the air, water and food safe (added later).

The Constitution of the United States

Preamble

We the People of the United States, in Order to form a more perfect Union, establish Justice, insure domestic Tranquility, provide for the common defense, promote the general Welfare, and secure the Blessings of Liberty to ourselves and our Posterity, do ordain and establish this Constitution for the United States of America.

Summary of the Articles of the Constitution

Article I

Lists rules for forming and running Congress, the law-making branch of government. Divides Congress into two houses, the Senate and the House of Representatives, and sets out the duties of each house. Lists the powers of the federal government.

Article II

Calls for a President to carry out the nation's laws. Describes procedures for electing the President and lists the President's powers.

Article III

Establishes a Supreme Court. Defines, and sets out laws for dealing with treason against the United States.

Article IV

Forbids any state from treating a citizen of another state differently from its own citizens. Gives Congress the power to admit new states to the Union.

Article V

Lists steps for amending (adding to or changing) the Constitution. Changes approved by at least three-fourths of the states become law.

Article VI

Makes the new Constitution the supreme law of the land, and requires all Federal and state officials to support it.

Article VII

Establishes that if at least nine states ratify the Constitution of 1787, it is considered the law of the land.

3. Decide what a law means.
    a. Settle arguments when people disagree.
    b. Decide what to do if people don't obey the law.

"A more perfect union" is in the **preamble**, or opening, of the *Constitution*. The first three words of the preamble, "We the People," announce that the *Constitution* is for all Americans.

> "We the People of the United States, in Order to form a more perfect Union, establish Justice, insure **domestic Tranquility**, provide for the common defense, promote the general Welfare, and secure the Blessings of Liberty to ourselves and our **Posterity**, do ordain and establish this Constitution for the United States of America."

Not everyone liked the *Constitution*. Nine of the 13 states had to ratify, or approve, it before it could become the law. Arguments in the states were worse than the terrible arguments at the Convention.

People who approved of the *Constitution* were called Federalists. Some, like Alexander Hamilton of New York, wrote newspaper articles explaining how the *Constitution* would work, and urged people to ratify it. James Madison and John Jay also wrote articles supporting the *Constitution*. These articles are known as *The Federalist Papers*.

The Anti-Federalists were people who disagreed with Hamilton, Madison and Jay. These people were afraid that the *Constitution* would create a central government so strong that it could endanger the rights of "life, liberty and the pursuit of happiness" for which thousands of Americans had fought and died. The arguments between the Federalists and Anti-Federalists continued for years.

Again, a compromise was necessary. The compromise added 10 **amendments** to the *Constitution*. These amendments persuaded most people to ratify *the Constitution*. There are now 27 amendments, but the *Constitution* began with 10. These first 10 amendments are called the ***Bill of Rights***, because they clearly state Americans' most important rights (see Appendix D).

The *Constitution* also says citizens have responsibilities. Americans must:

*   Vote to choose their leaders.
*   Pay taxes, so the government can do its job.
*   Serve on a **jury** when called.

The *Bill of Rights* protects freedoms and rights, including:

*   *Freedom of speech.* Americans have the freedom to express themselves and their beliefs, and to speak freely against their leaders.

Summary of the Amendments to the Constitution

*The first ten amendments make up the
Bill of Rights, adopted in 1791*

Amendment I

*Guarantees freedom of religion, of
speech, and of the press. Gives the
people the right to meet peaceably
and the right to voice complaints to
the government.*

Amendment II

*Says that states need to have groups of
people ready to protect themselves, so
therefore people can own guns.*

Amendment III

*Says the government cannot force
you to let soldiers stay in your home
during peacetime.*

Amendment IV

*Guarantees the right to privacy. Says
the government needs a good reason
to think you broke the law before it can
search you or your house or take away
your belongings.*

Amendment V

*Says the government must follow
certain rules when it accuses someone
of a crime. Forbids punishment without
a trial. Guarantees compensation if
property is taken by the government for
public use.*

Amendment VI

*Guarantees the right for people accused
of crimes to a speedy, fair trial by jury.*

Amendment VII

*Says if two people go to court to settle a
disagreement, they can have a jury trial
if the value is more than twenty dollars.*

Amendment VIII

*Says people accused of crimes have a
chance to get out of jail before trial.*

Amendment IX

*The people hold more rights than only
those listed in the Constitution.*

Amendment X

*Says the states have all powers that
the Constitution does not either give
to the U.S. government or take away
from the states.*

Summary of the Amendments to the Constitution (cont'd)

Amendment XI (1789)
Keeps any one of the states from being sued by citizens of another state or of a foreign country.

Amendment XII (1804)
Establishes presidential election procedures.

Amendment XIII (1865)
Forbids laws that unfairly deny citizens' rights and guarantees equal protection under the law to all.

Amendment XV (1870)
Forbids depriving citizens of the right to vote because of race or color.

Amendment XVI (1913)
Authorizes an income tax.

Amendment XVII (1913)
Calls for senators to be elected by direct vote of the people.

Amendment XVIII (1919)
The prohibition Amendment. Forbids the manufacture or sale of liquor.

Amendment XIX (1920)
Grants women the right to vote.

Amendment XX (1933)
Starts presidential and congressional terms in January.

Amendment XXI (1933)
Repeals the Eighteenth Amendment.

Amendment XXII (1951)
Bars any President from serving more than two terms (eight years) .

Amendment XXIII (1961)
Gives residents of the District of Colombia (Washington, D.C.) the right to vote for President.

Amendment XXIV (1964)
It is illegal to have as a voting requirement that one must pay taxes.

Amendment XXV (1967)
Establishes rules for succession if a President cannot complete the term.

Amendment XXVI (1971)
Lowers the legal voting age to eighteen.

People sometimes disagree over whether freedom of speech means Americans are free to express themselves even in ways that offend or insult other people. However, if you take away freedom of speech in some cases, where do you stop?

- *Freedom of the press.* The media and publications are free to say almost anything, even criticize the government, if they believe or can prove that what they say is true.

- *Freedom of religion.* You can worship or not worship as you choose. No American is required by law to hold any specific religious beliefs.

- *The right to a fair trial.* The government must follow rules that protect people who are charged with crimes.

The *Bill of Rights*, however, did not apply to thousands of African-American slaves, who had no rights or freedoms. The word "slavery" did not appear in the *Constitution*. Some delegates to the Constitutional Convention were opposed to slavery, but they didn't insist on **abolition**, because it would have kept them from an agreement. One delegate said slavery was a decision that belonged to the states. This solution was acceptable enough to get the *Constitution* written and approved. Eventually, slavery would tear apart the country that the *Constitution* was supposed to hold together.

The First Government

George Washington was elected America's first president by a large **majority** of voters. He was trusted and admired by the people, and his picture is on the $1 bill today. He is on the least valuable bill because it is also the most common bill, the bill people see more than any other.

Washington is often called "the father of the country," because he dedicated so much of his life to serving the United States when it was so young. Not only did he help win the American War of Independence, but he also played an important role at the Constitutional Convention in helping to reach agreement. He governed fairly, but did not find it easy to be president. At the end of his first term, he accepted a second term only because he wanted to unite a country that was already on the edge of breaking apart. He refused a third term, starting a tradition that presidents would only serve two four-year terms. That tradition became law when the 22nd amendment to the *Constitution* was **adopted** in 1951.

Washington put a group of men in charge of running some parts of the government. We call this group the president's **Cabinet**. Thomas Jefferson and Alexander Hamilton were two of Washington's Cabinet members, and they disagreed about many ideas. They had very different ideas about who should run the country, and about what kind of country the United States should be.

Thomas Jefferson and Alexander Hamilton

Jefferson wrote in the *Declaration of Independence* that, "all men are created equal." Hamilton did not believe people were equal. He believed history showed that a strong, wealthy **minority** had always **dominated** a weak majority. He wanted a strong federal government that would help businessmen by establishing a national bank, and by taxing imported **goods**. Hamilton pictured a future nation of prosperous businessmen, big cities and a strong federal government.

On the other hand, Jefferson was **suspicious** of big financial institutions. He thought it would be dangerous to have so much money under the control of one big bank. Jefferson imagined a **republic** of independent farmers. He believed in hard-working, educated people. Jefferson thought strong state governments and a weak federal government would prevent federal **tyranny**. He was afraid that Hamilton's policies would create a wealthy ruling class that controlled a poor working class.

The different beliefs led to the creation of political parties. Political parties, and the disagreements between them, are still part of democracy in America. Today, the two main political parties, Republicans and Democrats, usually disagree about how the government should be run. Sometimes these disagreements make it hard for the government to accomplish anything. Americans think this is still better than a single, all-powerful ruler (with whom no one dares to disagree) running everything.

The new country needed a capital. The city of Washington was chosen because it was halfway between the North and South. The District of Columbia was created so that the nation's capital would not be part of any one state. The **Capitol** building where Congress could meet, and the house where the president would live—the White House—were built in the 1790s. Washington, D.C. has many huge, stone government offices, magnificent museums and a spectacular library—the Library of Congress—where one can find almost every book. There are also many great monuments, including three that honor the great leaders—Washington, Jefferson and Lincoln.

Thomas Jefferson was only 33 years old when he wrote the *Declaration of Independence*. Later in 1801, he was elected the third president of the country. He believed in the value of a good education, and founded the University of Virginia. He studied mathematics, science, geography and music. Jefferson also studied architecture, and designed his own house—Monticello—which set the style for much of American architecture until the Civil War, about 60 years later.

During Jefferson's **presidency**, the United States completed the Louisiana Purchase in 1803. Jefferson bought the land from France that stretched from the Gulf of Mexico to Canada, and more than doubled the size of the United States.

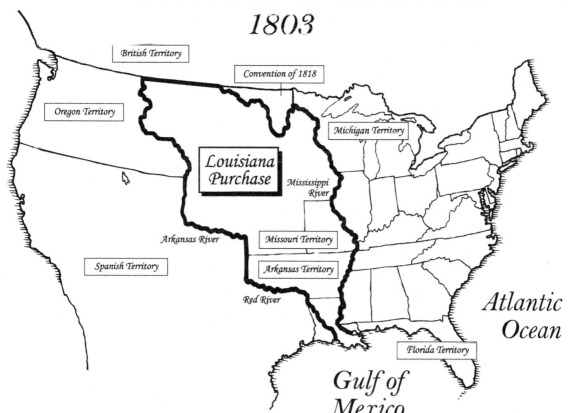

Louisiana Purchase
1803

British Territory

Convention of 1818

Oregon Territory

Michigan Territory

Louisiana Purchase

Mississippi River

Arkansas River

Missouri Territory

Spanish Territory

Arkansas Territory

Red River

Florida Territory

Atlantic Ocean

Gulf of Mexico

This part of the continent was unknown, so President Jefferson chose two men, Meriwether Lewis and William Clark, to explore it. They led an **expedition** from St. Louis, Missouri up the Missouri River, across the Rocky Mountains and down the Columbia River to the Pacific Ocean. The explorers met with many **hardships** on this difficult journey. They also met Sacagawea, a Native American teenager with a new baby. She helped them get to their destination. Not only did they make it to the Pacific Ocean, the explorers also established good relations with all of the Indians—thanks to Sacagawea.

Lewis and Clark and Sacagawea on the Journey to the Pacific Ocean

As the fourth president, James Madison had his hands full with many problems. In the West, Americans were angry because the British were encouraging Native American tribes, led by Tecumseh, to attack the settlers.

Britain was at war with France again, and both sides were interfering with American merchant ships. The British made Americans especially angry by "pressing" American sailors—pulling them off if their ships and forcing them to help the British fight against France.

Angry congressmen demanded that America declare war on Britain because of these British actions. These "war hawks" pushed President Madison to declare war in 1812, but they also had another motive. They wanted to take over Canada, the vast British-owned **territory** north of the United States. The United States lacked soldiers and supplies for the War of 1812. Congress was willing to talk about battling Britain, but it was not willing to tax the American people to pay for it. American troops lost many battles. It quickly became clear that America could not take Canada from the British.

In August 1814, the British attacked Washington, D.C., and set fire to the White House. Dolly Madison, the president's wife, saved a famous portrait of George Washington just before the British arrived with their torches. After the British burned the White House, they tried to capture nearby Baltimore, Maryland.

Francis Scott Key, a lawyer working a prisoner exchange on a British warship, watched the Americans hold Baltimore's Fort McHenry against heavy **shelling**. After the Americans were victorious and the smoke cleared over the fort, he saw the American flag still flying. Key wrote a poem called the *Star-Spangled Banner* that later provided the words to the **national anthem**.

The Star-Spangled Banner

Oh, say can you see by the dawn's early light
What so proudly we hailed at the twilight's last gleaming?
Whose broad stripes and bright stars thru the perilous fight,
O'er the ramparts we watched were so gallantly streaming?
And the rocket's red glare, the bombs bursting in air,
Gave proof through the night that our flag was still there.
Oh, say does that star-spangled banner yet wave
O'er the land of the free and the home of the brave?

On the shore, dimly seen through the mists of the deep,
Where the foe's haughty host in dread silence reposes,
What is that which the breeze, o'er the towering steep,
As it fitfully blows, half conceals, half discloses?
Now it catches the gleam of the morning's first beam,
In full glory reflected now shines in the stream:
'Tis the star-spangled banner! Oh long may it wave
O'er the land of the free and the home of the brave!

And where is that band who so vauntingly swore
That the havoc of war and the battle's confusion,
A home and a country should leave us no more!
Their blood has washed out their foul footsteps' pollution.
No refuge could save the hireling and slave
From the terror of flight, or the gloom of the grave:
And the star-spangled banner in triumph doth wave
O'er the land of the free and the home of the brave!

Oh! thus be it ever, when freemen shall stand
Between their loved home and the war's desolation!
Blest with victory and peace, may the heav'n rescued land
Praise the Power that hath made and preserved us a nation.
Then conquer we must, when our cause it is just,
And this be our motto: "In God is our trust."
And the star-spangled banner in triumph shall wave
O'er the land of the free and the home of the brave!

~ Francis Scott Key

The Battle at Fort McHenry

The fighting continued until December 24, 1814, when the two exhausted countries signed a peace treaty. America and Britain would never go to war again against each other. In fact, they fought as allies in later wars. The war did, however, make it clear to the world that the United States was a free and independent nation.

First Expansion of the United States

President James Monroe established new, expanded borders on both the north and south sides of the United States. As a result of an agreement with Great Britain, he established the border between the United States and Canada from Michigan to the Rocky Mountains, at the 49th **parallel**.

In the South, in 1818, he sent General Andrew Jackson to fight American Indians in Florida, which was still a colony of Spain. Some Americans were angry with the Seminole Indians in Florida, because they gave **refuge** to runaway slaves.

General Jackson and his troops burned the Seminole villages, but then the soldiers didn't leave. The Spanish government did not like having American troops in the Spanish colony. President Monroe used the troops to pressure Spain to sell Florida to the United States for $5 million.

While the United States was expanding its borders, other New World countries were beginning their struggle for independence from the Old World. Shortly after the United States won its independence from Britain, Spain's colonies in Latin America began fighting—and winning—independence. Since the Americans had so recently battled for independence, they sympathized with their Latin American neighbors.

President Monroe warned the European countries in his *Monroe Doctrine* not to interfere with the New World and if any European country did interfere in the New World, the U.S. would consider this an unfriendly act. In return, he said, America would not interfere in European wars or politics.

Andrew Jackson was a headstrong, stubborn general. He was cruel to Native Americans, but he was so popular that Americans elected him president in 1828. He was popular because many people saw him as a self-made man who succeeded through his own efforts, not because he was born rich or with any special advantages. President Jackson brought his rough, frontier ways to Washington, D.C.

At his inaugural celebration, (this official ceremony is held at the beginning of a presidency) farmers came from as far away as western Pennsylvania and Tennessee to cheer their hero. Many of these "backwoodsmen" pushed their way into a party at the White House. More polite senators and their wives were shocked to see farmers in muddy boots standing on the satin-covered cushions to catch a glimpse of the president.

Many Americans dreamed about expanding the country again, to create a nation that stretched "from sea to shining sea." Jackson helped make this dream come true. The American dream had a dark side. It was a nightmare for Native Americans who already lived where Americans wanted to go. Jackson agreed with many white Americans who thought American Indians were **savages**.

In 1830, President Jackson urged Congress to pass the Indian Removal **Act**, so he could force the Native Americans from their land, and give it to white settlers. Not everyone approved of Jackson's harsh plan. Almost half of the House of Representatives voted against the **bill**. Even though many disagreed, the bill passed, and the U.S. government began to force Native American tribes to move, sometimes more than a thousand miles from their

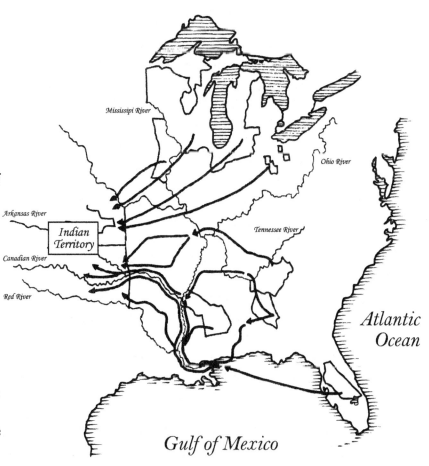

Effects of the Indian Removal Act
1830-1840s

Mississipi River

Ohio River

Arkansas River

Tennessee River

Indian Territory

Canadian River

Red River

Atlantic Ocean

Gulf of Mexico

land and homes. Most were moved to Indian Territory in what now is the state of Oklahoma.

One southeastern tribe, the Cherokee, refused to go. U.S. soldiers armed with rifles and **bayonets** put the Cherokee men, women and children (from Georgia, Tennessee and the Carolinas) into steamboats and railroad cars in the winter of 1838. The Cherokee had to walk the last 800 miles of their journey to Oklahoma—a path now called the Trail of Tears. Most had few clothes, and no shoes or **moccasins**. About 4,000 of the 16,000 Cherokee people died of **starvation**, cold and disease on this terrible journey.

In Florida, the Seminoles, under their strong warrior leader, Osceola, also fought being **uprooted**. After two years of fighting, Osceola agreed to meet with an American general to discuss a peace treaty, but the meeting was a trap. Osceola was captured and later died in prison.

Americans traveled west to these new lands along two main routes. The Santa Fe Trail started at Independence, Missouri and ran south to the Mexican province of New Mexico. The Oregon Trail to the northwest also started at Independence, Missouri, but ran north to Boise, Idaho and then continued on to Oregon. Pioneer families often traveled these routes in big covered wagons called prairie schooners.

Many Americans in the 1830s and 1840s believed in an idea called "manifest destiny," which means something that is clearly and obviously supposed to happen. People believed that God wanted Americans to keep moving west until the United States reached from the Atlantic Ocean to the Pacific Ocean.

Americans were moving into the old Spanish colony (now part of Texas) and created a government of their own and they wanted to be separate from Mexico. The United States also claimed a vast stretch of land north of the Rio Grande River, which the Mexicans said belonged to them. These actions **sparked** the Mexican-American war. As usual for Americans, many people supported the war while others strongly opposed it. There were many battles with Mexico over this land **issue**. One of the most important ones took place at the Alamo Mission in San Antonio in 1836. All of the Americans defending the fort were killed.

Americans thought they would quickly defeat Mexico, but they didn't. The war finally ended when American troops defeated the Mexican soldiers who were defending Mexico City and captured General Antonio López de Santa Anna. Mexico lost more in the war than just the land north of the Rio Grande. The United States gained about 500,000 square miles of territory, including what are now the states of California, Nevada and Utah; and parts of Colorado, New Mexico and Arizona.

American Trails West 1860

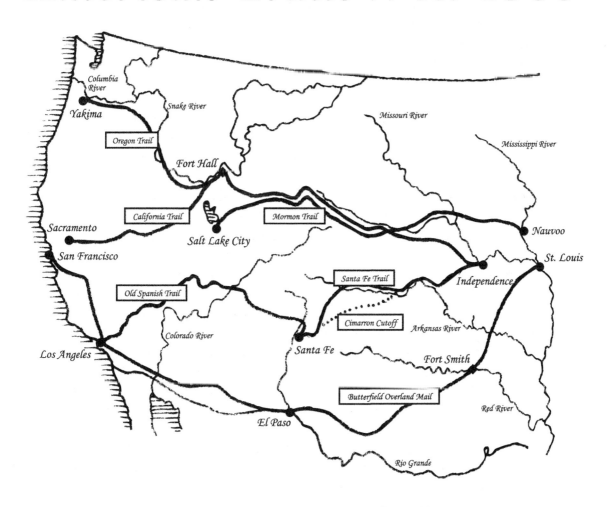

Prairie Schooners in a Wagon Train Going West

After the war, Texas established itself as an independent republic with its own president and government. While the U.S. recognized the Lone Star Republic (Texas), it did not immediately approve its request to join the U.S. Congress was concerned about the balance of slave states versus free states (Texas was a slave state) in the government and it didn't want another war with Mexico. Finally, after much discussion, Texas became a state in 1845.

Reform in the United States

In the 1820s and 1830s, many people saw things wrong with American society, and tried to reform them—to make them right. Some of these people worked for better care for the mentally ill, and for better schools. Others tried to change people's behavior and **morals**.

Dorothea Dix was 14 when she became a schoolteacher in Massachusetts. She taught for many years, and wrote children's books. She is remembered mostly, however, for helping the mentally ill. It all started by chance. In 1841, Dix volunteered to teach a **Sunday school** class at a Massachusetts jail.

She was shocked by what she saw. People who had not committed any crime were locked up with **criminals** because they were mentally ill. They were locked in rooms with no heat. They were treated no better than animals.

Better treatment for the mentally ill became Dix's greatest **cause**. She traveled all over Massachusetts, visiting jails and houses for the poor. Dix pushed the government for new or **renovated** hospitals for the mentally ill.

Horace Mann wanted to improve education. There was a lot to improve. The rich had **access** to good private schools. Most schools, however, were small, chilly, one-room buildings, with very few books. Teachers earned very low pay. Many were not even trained to be teachers.

Most children could only attend school for a few years, and then had to work to help support their families. When they did go to school, they could only attend for three or four months of the year because they had to spend summers working on their farms. This is why many American students still don't have school in the summer.

Mann believed in universal education—all children should learn to read and write and become good citizens. As the leader of the first Board of Education in Massachusetts, Mann had more schools built, lengthened the school year to at least six months, and got better pay for teachers. Massachusetts established the first college to train teachers.

Supporters of the **temperance** movement wanted people to stop drinking alcohol. Too many men spent all their money at the saloon, rather than buying food and clothes for their children.

In the 1800s, women were expected not to take an active role in society. Many women, and some men, thought women should have the same rights and opportunities as men. These people were called feminists.

Margaret Fuller was a feminist writer. She taught women things that had nothing to do with housekeeping—Greek mythology, for example, or **fine arts**. In her book, *Woman in the Nineteenth Century*, Fuller said women could perform any job. Women couldn't vote then, or attend most colleges. They couldn't hold most jobs, so they couldn't earn much money.

Women did hold some jobs—low-paid factory workers, teachers and office helpers—but they usually couldn't be managers or bosses. All of the property and money in a family belonged to the husband, even if the wife earned some or all of it.

Many reformers in the North wanted to end slavery. They were called **abolitionists**. These abolitionists formed the American Anti-Slavery Society in the 1830s. Women played a significant role in this movement as well.

One Room Schoolhouse

Two abolitionists, Lucretia Mott and Elizabeth Cady Stanton, made the long trip across the Atlantic to speak at an important anti-slavery meeting in London, but they were not allowed to participate. They were told to sit quietly while the men spoke. Later, Mott and Stanton helped organize a meeting of about 100 women and men to discuss women's rights in Seneca Falls, New York in July 1848. Urging women to speak their minds was a dramatic move. Proper women weren't supposed to speak in public. Frederick Douglass and Sojourner Truth, former slaves who had become great abolitionists, attended.

The people who gathered at Seneca Falls wrote their ideas of women's rights into a *Declaration of Sentiments*. It was modeled after the *Declaration of Independence*. It announced, "We hold these truths to be self-evident: that all men and women are created equal." The

WOMEN WIN RIGHT TO VOTE IN SUFFRAGETTE VICTORY

Women Suffragettes Marching for the Right to Vote

document attacked the traditional promise that a woman made when she married—to love, honor, and *obey* her husband. This promise seemed to the people at Seneca Falls to force women into a kind of slavery. The most shocking part of the declaration was demanding that women be allowed to vote. Some newspapers called the idea "ridiculous" and "evil."

Elizabeth Cady Stanton joined another determined **advocate** for women's rights: Susan B. Anthony. Stanton and Anthony helped found the National Woman Suffrage Association. (Suffrage is the right to vote.)

Throughout the late 1800s, Stanton and Anthony gave speeches and organized **petitions** in favor of a constitutional amendment that would give women the right to vote. In 1872, Anthony was **arrested** for voting in the presidential election. At the trial, she told the judge that she was rebelling against man-made, unjust and **unconstitutional** laws. To honor her achievements in this area, Anthony became the first woman pictured on an American coin—a silver dollar—in 1979 (Sacagawea became the second woman on an American coin in 2000).

The demand for women's rights grew stronger as America entered the 20th century. Finally, in 1920, the 19th Amendment was added to the *Constitution*. It says: "The rights of citizens of the United States to vote shall not be denied or **abridged** by the United States or by any State on account of sex."

Other events were also shaping America. A potato **famine** in Ireland forced a wave of emigrants to leave Ireland to live in the U.S. Other groups of people came from all over the world for political and religious reasons. The discovery of gold in California in 1849 started a **surge** to the west. The Homestead Act of 1862 gave 160 acres to each **homesteader** who lived on the land and farmed it. That opened the **floodgates** of Western settlement.

At the same time, American society was increasingly divided over the issue of slavery. This issue would tear the country in half—North against South—in the bloodiest war in United States history: the Civil War.

A Nation Divided
1850-1870

Trouble with Self-Government

In the mid-1800s, American population and industry were booming, but the country was growing apart.

The North was becoming industrialized. Northern factories made iron, steel, machinery and cloth. Canals and railroads made the Northeast the country's center for business and trade. Since farmers were using more machines and needed fewer workers, people moved to the cities for jobs.

The South had better weather for farming, so the Southern economy was heavily agricultural. It depended on workers, not machines. The most profitable crop—cotton—was grown on large plantations that depended on slave labor, while the smaller Southern farms were worked without slaves. At mid-century, slaves in the South made up about four-fifths of the skilled labor and performed the hardest work. An entire way of life developed that depended on slavery.

Until the 1830s, many Southerners criticized slavery. Prominent Southern leaders, including Thomas Jefferson of Virginia, were uneasy about it. Some, including Jefferson, objected to it on moral grounds, even though they owned slaves. Abolition, however, would force them to give up their way of life.

Slavery had existed in the North in colonial times, but it was not as necessary as industry developed. More people made their living as small farmers, shopkeepers, craftsmen and factory workers. Many

A Slave Working on a Southern Cotton Plantation

Northerners began to oppose slavery. They considered it morally wrong, and a threat to the basic principles of democracy. This difference of opinion on slavery began to drive the nation toward war.

More territories became **eligible** to become states, or join the Union, as more people moved west in the early 19th century. The South wanted the new states to allow slavery, while the North did not. The issue was important because if either side gained a majority in Congress, it could pass laws against the wishes of the other side.

In 1819, the United States had 11 slave states and 11 free states. Then, Missouri applied to become a new slave state. This **triggered** long, angry **debates** in Congress. An agreement called the Missouri Compromise was finally reached in 1820. Maine was admitted as a free state, and to balance that, Missouri was admitted to the Union as a slave state.

This balancing act was part of a larger agreement. Congress decided that the Mason-Dixon Line, which ran along the Maryland-Pennsylvania border, would be the new **boundary**. All of the territory north of the east-west line, except Missouri, would be free, while settlers south of the line could own slaves. **According to** the *Constitution*, the states were supposed to strive to become a "more perfect union," with many states united in one country. The Missouri Compromise was a dangerous agreement that seemed to divide the country in two.

The **Fugitive** Slave Act made it very difficult for slaves to run away to freedom. Slaves were not **entitled** to a trial by jury if they were **accused** of a crime, and were returned to their owners if they ran away. Then, they were usually whipped or hanged.

Abolitionists created a secret escape route called the Underground Railroad to help escaped slaves. These escaped slaves could use safe houses as they traveled north to freedom. One of the most famous "conductors," or guides, was former slave Harriet Tubman.

Harriet Beecher Stowe's 1852 **novel** *Uncle Tom's Cabin* helped concentrate Northern feelings about slavery. More than 300,000 copies of *Uncle Tom's Cabin* sold in one year—a huge number of books for that time. In the book, Uncle Tom was a kind and loyal slave. He saved the life of a white child, but was eventually sold to a cruel master, Simon Legree. After Uncle Tom refused to **betray** two escaped slaves, Simon Legree whipped him to death. Some Northern readers were so angry after they read the book that they wanted to force an end to slavery.

An 1857 Supreme Court decision on the Dred Scott case pushed the North and South even closer to war. Dred Scott was a slave. His owner moved from the slave state of Missouri to the free territory of Wisconsin. Scott got married there and had two daughters. Then, Scott's owner moved back to Missouri, taking Scott and his family with him as slaves. Scott argued in court that he and his family were free, because they had lived in a free territory, and the children had been born there.

The Supreme Court, with most of the justices from the South, used the case to make a pro-slavery stand. It ruled that it didn't matter where Scott had lived, slaves were property, and owners could take their property and their children wherever they wanted. The chief justice, like many people, decided that the declaration that "all men are created equal" did not apply to slaves. The court also declared the Missouri Compromise unconstitutional. It said that Congress had no right to exclude slavery from

Dred Scott in the Witness Box at Court

any territory. Soon, Scott's owner sold Dred Scott and his family, and they were freed by another owner.

Slavery dominated the 1858 senatorial election in Illinois. Senator Stephen A. Douglas ran for re-election to the U.S. Senate against Abraham "Honest Abe" Lincoln.

Lincoln was a member of the newly founded Republican Party, which strongly opposed slavery. In an 1858 speech, Lincoln warned that, "I believe this government cannot endure permanently, half slave and half free." Lincoln challenged Douglas to a series of debates on slavery. Douglas said that white men in each state or territory should be allowed to decide if they wanted to allow slavery. Lincoln argued that the country must take a moral stand against it.

Douglas defeated Lincoln. Lincoln, however, also won a sort of victory. The tall, thin, **self-educated** country lawyer who argued against slavery gained national attention in the debates, which put him on the road to the presidency.

The year before the 1860 presidential election, a violent slave **uprising** frightened Southern slaveholders. An abolitionist named John Brown believed so strongly in freedom for blacks that he was willing to use violence to gain their freedom. In October 1859, Brown led 18 men, including five free African-Americans, in an attempt to capture weapons at Harpers Ferry, Virginia. He planned to **arm** the slaves for a rebellion, but his plan failed. He was wounded, captured and hanged. Southerners were furious when Northerners called Brown a hero, because the Southerners considered him a dangerous **fanatic**.

Many Southerners believed that the North would fight the South over slavery. They began to argue that the only way to protect the South and its way of life was to secede (break away) from the United States. Southerners believed that states had the right to decide whether to allow slavery or not, because the *Constitution* did not prohibit slavery.

One of the central issues in the Lincoln's presidential **campaign** was opposition to the spread of slavery. So many Southerners were **appalled** when Lincoln was **narrowly** elected president in 1860, even though he failed to win a single Southern state. They considered Lincoln's election proof that the North was their enemy, so the Southern states took the dangerous step of leaving the Union.

South Carolina became the first state to secede in December 1860. By February 1861, six more states in the South had seceded (Mississippi, Florida, Alabama, Georgia, Louisiana and Texas). When Lincoln was inaugurated in March 1861, five states in the upper South still had not seceded: Virginia, Arkansas, North Carolina, Tennessee and Kentucky.

Some people in these states opposed slavery, but didn't want to fight their Southern neighbors. Some Northerners believed that the Southern states which had seceded should be allowed to leave the United States. A war, they said, would just hurt the North.

The Civil War began on the morning of April 12, 1861, at Fort Sumter, which was located on an island off South Carolina. Southerners wanted U.S. soldiers to leave the South. Fort Sumter was running out of supplies, but it was one of the few forts in the South still manned by Union soldiers.

The United States when the Civil War Began

Dakota Territory

Nebraska Territory

Union States

Indian Territory

Confederate States

Atlantic Ocean

Gulf of Mexico

Lincoln knew the South would probably resist any attempt to re-supply the fort. He sent them anyway. When the Southerners heard that supply ships were on the way, they started bombing Fort Sumter.

Lincoln called up a Union (Northern) Army to halt the South's "rebellious ways." The South, he said, had fired the first shots. The Southerners argued they were forced to fire first because of Lincoln's actions. Who started it really didn't matter because the Civil War had been brewing for years.

Shortly after the attack on Fort Sumter, Virginia seceded from the Union, quickly followed by three other southern states (Arkansas, North Carolina and Tennessee). The four remaining slave states remained in the Union (Maryland, Delaware, Kentucky and Missouri). In all, 11 states seceded from the Union to form the Confederate States of America. Their name was a **reminder** of the colonial *Articles of Confederation*. Each side expected a quick victory. They were both horribly wrong.

After Fort Sumter was defeated, President Lincoln sought 75,000 volunteers to join the army and save the Union. The southern Confederate states planned to raise an army of about 100,000 men. Before the Civil War was over, the Union sent more than two million Union soldiers in blue uniforms to war against almost one million Confederates in gray uniforms.

Few of the men on either side had firsthand experience of the horrors of war. They weren't thinking about bloodshed and death. They romanticized war as an adventure, with exciting battles and brave heroes. In Washington, D.C., some people were so excited about the war that on July 21, 1861, they packed picnic baskets and sat on the hillsides above the first major battle, like spectators at a football game. Union troops attacked Confederate troops along a creek called Bull Run, near Manassas, Virginia (about 30 miles west of Washington, D.C.).

At first it looked like the Union soldiers were winning, but then Confederate Gen. Thomas J. Jackson arrived with reinforcements. His troops held their ground "like a stone wall," earning the general the nickname "Stonewall" Jackson. Confederate troops then attacked the Union soldiers, who fled, along with the frightened sightseers. The Confederates won.

Bull Run, however, was just the beginning of a long and deadly Civil War. More Americans died in the Civil War than in any war, before or since. Between 620,000 and 750,000 Americans died in the war. Confederates would continue to win most of the major battles from 1861 to the summer of 1863.

In 1861, many Southerners wanted the Confederacy to exist as no more than a loose collection of states, with a weak central government.

The Confederate states adopted a constitution with strong rules favoring slavery and states' rights.

Just 100 miles from Washington, D.C., the Confederate government established a capital at Richmond, Virginia, and elected Jefferson Davis president. Davis had been an American congressman and senator, as well as secretary of war for the 14th president, Franklin Pierce. Davis was not an effective leader and he was often ill. At the beginning of the war, most Southerners considered Davis a hero, but eventually, Confederate leaders blamed Davis for the South's losses.

About one in every four Union soldiers was an **immigrant**. Men of all ages became soldiers—from 9 years old to 80. Most soldiers were young men, but some were just boys. The boy soldiers usually didn't fight. They carried food and water, took care of the horses and did other **chores**. Boy soldiers filled two other important roles, as buglers and drummers. Civil War soldiers depended upon the sound of the bugle or drums to tell them when to wake up, when to attack and when to retreat. On a battlefield dark with gun smoke, drums told a soldier where to go and what to do.

Gen. Robert E. Lee commanded the Confederate army. A **graduate** of the U.S. military academy at West Point, Lee served in the United States Army for more than 30 years. He was a hero of the Mexican-American War. Lee led the federal troops that halted John Brown's **raid**.

Lee had to make a painful decision when the Civil War broke out. He was from Virginia, but felt strong loyalty to the Union. A few days after the attack on Fort Sumter, Lee was asked to take command of all Union forces. He could not fight his family and his home. Lee **resigned** from the Union Army, and joined the Confederate army.

The First Battle of Bull Run

Lee was President Davis's top military adviser by the spring of 1862. Lee was a master planner and strong leader in battle after battle. Soldiers who served under Lee liked and respected him. He set a good example—he did not **curse**, smoke or drink alcohol.

The first years of the war were discouraging for the Union side. President Lincoln replaced several of the generals in charge of Union troops, looking for someone who could win. Several officers began to prove themselves. Ulysses S. Grant had also attended West Point. He and Lee

Ulysses S. Grant and Robert E. Lee

fought in the Mexican-American War. However, Grant and Lee had little in common. Not only was Grant 15 years younger than Lee, he sometimes drank too much alcohol. When the Civil War began, Grant wasn't even in the military—he had left to work in his father's leather shop in Illinois.

As soon as he learned of the attack on Fort Sumter, Grant organized local volunteers. He joined the war as a colonel in charge of the Illinois **regiment** of about 1,000 soldiers. President Lincoln soon promoted him to general. As general, Grant led the Union to its first important victory. In February 1862, his Union troops captured Fort Henry and Fort Donelson in Tennessee. When the Confederate commander at Fort Donelson realized his troops were outnumbered, he sent Grant a message asking for the **terms** of surrender. Grant sent back a message saying, "No terms except an unconditional and immediate surrender can be accepted."

After fighting for three days, the Confederates at Fort Donelson finally surrendered. Northerners joked that Grant's initials (U.S.G.) stood for "Unconditional Surrender Grant." Lincoln had finally found the general who could win. By the beginning of 1864, Lincoln had placed Grant in charge of the entire Union Army.

When the war began, President Lincoln insisted that the war was not being fought over slavery but to save the Union. Lincoln also wanted to **abolish** slavery, but first he said he wanted to reunite the nation. He had to be careful about what he said against slavery, because some states fighting on the Union side allowed slavery—the "border" states of Delaware, Maryland, Kentucky and Missouri. Lincoln was worried that, if he took too strong a stand against slavery, the border states would join the Confederacy.

Northerners who opposed slavery urged President Lincoln to abolish slavery. He refused, but in spring 1862 Congress began to pass laws against slavery without his approval. President Lincoln then became convinced that freeing the slaves would help the Union win the war. He issued the *Emancipation Proclamation.* "Emancipate" means to set free. A "proclamation" is an official statement.

The *Emancipation Proclamation* announced that all slaves in the U.S., including the Confederacy, would be free beginning January 1, 1863. In 1865, Lincoln convinced lawmakers to pass the 13th Amendment to abolish slavery throughout the nation. However, neither Congress nor President Lincoln could force Southern slave owners to free their slaves immediately. News of the *Emancipation Proclamation* gave hope and joy to African-Americans still in slavery.

In both the Revolutionary War and the War of 1812, African-Americans fought bravely, but neither the Union nor the Confederacy allowed African-Americans to serve as soldiers at the beginning of the war. Many whites in both the North and the South thought blacks were not smart enough or brave enough to be good soldiers.

Even though they weren't allowed to fight as soldiers, African-Americans still helped the Union. Some spied on Confederate troops. Harriet Tubman was one of many who **sneaked** behind the battle lines to try to get important information about Confederate armies. The Union Army had **drafted** thousands of white men (many of whom did not want to fight) because not enough soldiers were joining. In the summer of 1862, the Union finally allowed blacks to become soldiers, and many rushed to volunteer. The *Emancipation Proclamation* encouraged more blacks to join the Union cause. By the end of the war, one in 10 Union soldiers, and one in four Union sailors, were African-American.

The first Union Army regiment composed of African-American troops was the 54th Massachusetts Volunteer Infantry Regiment. Colonel Robert Gould Shaw, a young white officer and the son of an abolitionist believed in his black troops. The African-Americans also believed in themselves. In July 1863, the 54th finally went into battle near Charleston, South Carolina and defeated a rebel charge. Days later, however, the 54th experienced a much tougher test. It was ordered to attack Fort Wagner, which was a huge Confederate **fortress** with thick walls and powerful guns.

The 54th charged the fort. Shaw and a black flag bearer, Sergeant W.H. Carney, braved heavy gun and cannon fire to race to the top of a wall. Carney fell, wounded, but caught the flag before it touched the ground. Shaw shouted back to his troops, "Rally, 54th! Rally!" Then, Shaw was shot in the heart by a Confederate bullet. He fell over dead and **toppled** from the fort's wall. Almost half the men of the 54th died in the attempt to take Fort Wagner. The fort remained in Confederate hands, but the soldiers of the 54th had proven that African-Americans were capable of great courage and sacrifice for their country.

Despite that, black soldiers were usually not treated as well as white soldiers. At first, African-Americans were paid less. Many black soldiers were angry about the "short pay" and refused to accept any wages at

Soldiers Fighting at the Battle of Fort Wagner

all until the government agreed to pay them the same as white soldiers. In June 1864, Congress passed a law requiring equal pay for all soldiers, regardless of color. Even so, blacks were usually not allowed to become officers. However, Major Martin R. Delany, an African-American, did become an officer and was the highest-ranking black soldier in the Union Army.

As the years of war passed, both soldiers and **civilians** learned that war doesn't mean glory—it means hunger, illness, suffering and death. The food the army gives soldiers is called "rations." It was rare for soldiers to have fresh meat or vegetables. Instead, they often ate cold salted pork, or perhaps some beans and a biscuit called "hardtack." This important item was so hard to chew that soldiers had to soak it in water or coffee or fry it in pork fat before they could eat it. If they were on the march, or if supply wagons were blocked, soldiers would go several days without any food.

Even though hardtack was bad, hungry Confederate soldiers might have gladly traded their rations for some Yankee food. Confederate soldiers just had hard black cakes of fried cornmeal called "pone."

Disease spread quickly since most doctors didn't understand that germs caused and spread disease. The soldiers saw nothing wrong with sharing a cup with a sick man or reusing a dirty bandage. Half of all troops were often too sick to fight. Surgery was **crude**. A severely wounded

Surgery on a Civil War Battlefield

or infected arm or leg was usually **amputated**. One in 13 Civil War soldiers returned home missing one or more arms and legs. For every three soldiers killed in battle, five more died of disease. In fact, diarrhea, which leads to **dehydration** and is no longer considered serious, was the leading cause of death during the war.

By the summer of 1863, the Confederacy still appeared to be winning, but the Union Army and Navy were attacking the Confederacy from all sides. The cities and forts all along the southern coastline were **bombarded** by the Union Navy. Finally, the Union controlled everything along the Mississippi River, except a single Confederate fort at Vicksburg, Mississippi. Grant's Union troops had surrounded it.

Most of the war had been fought on Southern soil. So, Lee tried to draw Grant north, away from Vicksburg. Lee led 75,000 troops from Virginia on a long march into Pennsylvania. On July 1, 1863, some of Lee's army approached Gettysburg, in southern Pennsylvania—only to be surprised by about 90,000 Union soldiers who were waiting for them. Lee's troops and **artillery** attacked for two days. Union troops had the advantage, because they were firing down at the Confederates from hilltops.

On the **stifling** hot afternoon of July 3, the Union cannons stopped firing, making the Confederates think the cannons had been destroyed.

It was a trick.

Lee ordered General George Edward Pickett and about 15,000 Confederate troops to make one massive attack. Pickett's men marched forward in orderly rows, as if on parade. They made easy targets for Union soldiers, who were **crouched** behind a stone wall with loaded guns. "Pickett's Charge" lasted only half an hour. Nearly half of the Confederate troops were killed.

The next day, July 4, 1863, on the country's birthday, Lee waited all day for the Union troops to attack his weary men. When the attack never came, Lee began the long retreat back to Virginia. Unfortunately, he did not know that earlier and 1,000 miles away, the Confederate fort at Vicksburg, Mississippi, had fallen to the Union troops led by Grant. Now the entire Mississippi River was under Union control.

Of the 151,000 men who fought at Gettysburg, more than 51,000 were killed, wounded or went missing—about 23,000 for the North, 28,000 for the South. The Union had finally defeated Lee's mighty army in a major battle. This marked a turning point. Although there were many months of fighting ahead, the Union started to think it could win.

To honor the soldiers who had fallen at Gettysburg, the governors of the Northern states created a national cemetery there, and asked President Lincoln to dedicate it. Speaking slowly and carefully, the president took just

The Gettysburg Address
November 19, 1863

Four score and seven years ago our fathers brought forth on this continent, a new nation, conceived in Liberty, and dedicated to the proposition that all men are created equal.

Now we are engaged in a great civil war, testing whether that nation or any nation so conceived and so dedicated, can long endure. We are met on a great battle-field of that war. We have come to dedicate a portion of that field, as a final resting place for those who here gave their lives that that nation might live. It is altogether fitting and proper that we should do this.

But, in a larger sense, we can not dedicate – we can not consecrate – we can not hallow – this ground. The brave men, living and dead, who struggled here, have consecrated it, far above our poor power to add or detract. The world will little note, nor long remember what we say here, but it can never forget what they did here. It is for us the living, rather, to be dedicated here to the unfinished work which they who fought here have thus far so nobly advanced. It is rather for us to be here dedicated to the great task remaining before us – that from these honored dead we take increased devotion to that cause for which they gave the last full measure of devotion – that we here highly resolve that these dead shall not have died in vain – that this nation, under God, shall have a new birth of freedom – and that government of the people, by the people, for the people, shall not perish from the earth.

over two minutes to deliver his speech which consisted of less than 275 well-chosen words. The Gettysburg **Address** has become one of the most famous speeches in American history.

In his speech, Lincoln echoed the *Declaration of Independence*. He reminded everyone present, and all Americans since, of the high ideals behind the founding of this country. The speech helped the country realize that it was not a collection of states, but one unified nation.

In the spring of 1864, Gen. William Tecumseh Sherman began to lead Union troops into the heart of the Confederacy. From May to mid-July 1864, Sherman's army battled to the **outskirts** of Atlanta, Georgia, one of the largest southern cities. By the end of the summer, Sherman's troops marched into Atlanta and forced the troops and civilians who lived there to flee.

When Union troops left later, they set fires that burned down much of the city. Sherman knew his actions were harsh, but believed that only suffering the horror of war would convince Southerners to surrender. During "Sherman's March to the Sea," his troops formed a line 60 miles wide, and destroyed every house, barn and field of crops in their path, from Atlanta to Savannah. Wherever Sherman's troops went, they left starving Southerners behind.

With the capture of Atlanta, more Northerners became convinced that the Union would win. In the 1864 presidential election, Northern voters showed their faith in Lincoln by re-electing him. By the spring of 1865, the end of the war was near.

Union troops controlled at least part of every state in the Confederacy. Tired, hungry Confederate troops had spent the cold winter in damp **trenches**, waiting for Grant to attack. Lee knew Grant would attack as soon as good spring weather arrived. Lee decided to surprise the Union troops by attacking in March, but they faced Grant's larger, better-supplied army.

Lee sent an urgent telegram to Jefferson Davis in the Confederate capital. On a Sunday morning, a messenger delivered the telegram to the church Davis was attending. Davis turned pale when he read the telegram. It said Richmond must be surrendered to the Yankees. Davis and other Confederate officials boarded trains heading to Danville, Virginia, where they hoped to establish a new capital. As they left, Confederates set fire to much of Richmond so that the Yankees wouldn't be able to use the city as a base.

On April 3, 1865, Union troops led by a group of black soldiers entered Richmond, Virginia. Crowds of cheering African-Americans, many of them former slaves, greeted them. The capital of the Confederacy had fallen. Lee's remaining troops were fleeing through Virginia, and Lee made it to a small town called Appomattox Court House.

Grant sent a note to Lee: "The results of the last week must convince you of the hopelessness of further resistance." Grant asked Lee to surrender so that further bloodshed could be stopped. Lincoln told Grant that the terms of surrender should be **generous**. So, Grant asked only that Lee's soldiers lay down their weapons and stop fighting until they could be exchanged for Union soldiers held by the Confederates.

Lee met Grant in the front room of a house in Appomattox Court House on April 9, 1865. Upon arrival, Grant and Lee shook hands. Grant tried to make Lee feel comfortable by talking about the time they fought together in the Mexican-American War. Lee solemnly interrupted and said it was time to discuss the terms of surrender.

Now that Grant had won, he was generous to Lee's troops. Grant agreed to let Lee's soldiers return to their homes. The Confederates had to give up their guns and military supplies, but Confederate officers were allowed to keep their horses and personal weapons. Lee was pleased with this unexpected kindness. However, he worried about the soldiers of lower rank, who had brought their own horses to the war. When Lee asked if

The Surrender at Appomattox Court House
and the End of the Civil War

they could also keep their horses, Grant promised, "to let all the men who claim to own a horse or mule take the animals home with them to work their little farms." Finally, Lee told Grant that his troops had no food. Grant immediately ordered his officers to send beef, bread, coffee and sugar to the hungry Confederates. For many of them, it was the first good meal they had eaten in months.

Once the generals agreed on the terms of surrender, Lee rose to leave. He shook hands with Grant, bowed to the other Union officers present, and left the room. Speaking to no one, he called for his beloved horse, Traveller, and rode away. Grant stood quietly on the porch and removed his hat as a sign of his respect for Lee. The other Union soldiers did the same. Union soldiers started to celebrate the surrender, but Grant silenced them. He did not want to **shame** the rebel soldiers. "The war is over," Grant said, "The rebels are our countrymen again."

A saddened Lee told his troops about the surrender. They were battle-hardened soldiers who had fought bravely, but many of them could not help crying. Lee's last orders were simple: "Boys, I have done the best I could for you. Go home now, and if you make as good citizens as you have soldiers, you will do well, and I shall always be proud of you."

The Civil War increased the federal government's power and authority. During the war, the federal government passed laws that gave them more control of individual citizens, for example, to use personal taxes to pay for the troops and the draft. The war increased economic growth, industry and farming in the North and Midwest, but destroyed most of the industry and farmland in the South. It would take the South years to recover.

Reunification and Growth 1870-1910

Transition Back to Self-Government

Northerners celebrated Lee's surrender. In Washington, D.C., crowds of people filled the streets outside the White House to cheer for President Lincoln, but the rejoicing would soon end. On April 14, 1865, President Lincoln and his wife attended a play at Ford's Theater, not far from the White House.

A Southern actor named John Wilkes Booth was also at Ford's Theater that night, but he wasn't on the stage. Booth believed in slavery and had supported the Confederacy. Booth sneaked up behind the president and shot Lincoln in the head as he sat watching the play. Booth ran from the theater and fled on a horse. Lincoln was quickly carried to a house across the street, but he didn't survive the night. He died early the next morning.

After **evading** the soldiers for a week, Booth was finally trapped in a barn in northern Virginia. When Booth refused to give himself up, soldiers set fire to the barn. Booth was shot and killed as he fled the flames.

Viewing of Lincoln's
Body in the Capitol

Joy at the end of the war turned to deep **mourning**. President Lincoln had steered the nation through its most difficult time. Even during the war, Lincoln

began planning "**reconstruction**," to ease the process of bringing the
11 Southern states back into the Union. Lincoln asked all Americans to
welcome the return of the Southern states "with **malice** toward none,
with **charity** for all." After the assassination, however, many Northerners
were still angry at Southerners, whom they considered traitors.

Within President Lincoln's Republican Party, a group disagreed with
Lincoln's plan to be kind to the Southern states. Radical Republicans
believed that white Southerners couldn't be trusted to treat blacks fairly.
The Radicals said the federal government must **guarantee** the rights of
freed African-Americans, including the right to vote.

Under the U.S. *Constitution*, when a president dies in office, the vice
president becomes president. After Lincoln died, Vice President Andrew
Johnson became president. Johnson, a native of North Carolina who had
been governor of Tennessee, owned slaves before the war. Johnson quickly
granted **amnesty** (forgiveness or pardon) to the Southerners. Most
Southerners received amnesty simply by **swearing** to be loyal to the
United States. Johnson wanted to quickly return control of the South to the
individual state governments. He agreed that slavery was still illegal, but he
wanted the states to decide what rights they would give African-Americans.

He said the Southern states had to amend their state constitutions
to abolish slavery and satisfy several other requirements. Then, they
would have the same rights and powers as any other state in the Union.
Most white Southerners liked Johnson's plan. Many of the Confederate
leaders who lost the war returned to state legislatures across the South,
and passed the Black Codes. These laws denied blacks their basic rights,
including the right to vote.

Black Codes limited African-Americans' ability to own property and
work in certain trades and businesses. Some of the laws gave whites the
right to treat black workers almost like slaves. It was as if the war had
not changed anything for blacks. The Black Codes convinced the Radical
Republicans in Congress that white Southerners could not be trusted, and
that Johnson's plan for Reconstruction had to be **overturned**.

In 1867, Congress passed laws that forced 10 of the 11 former
Confederate states to start Reconstruction over again. President Johnson
tried to block these laws by using his veto, but the Radicals in Congress had
enough votes to override Johnson's veto. These new laws required the 10
Confederate states to allow all men to vote, including blacks. These states
would remain under the control of the federal army until they satisfied all
of Congress's requirements. Many former Confederate leaders were no
longer allowed to hold **public office**. Federal military officials tried to
register blacks to vote.

With blacks voting, Republicans were elected to the state legislatures. This led to the creation of two **stereotypes**: "scalawags" and "carpetbaggers." White Southerners who didn't like the new state governments called people who cooperated with them scalawags, or **rascals**. Some scalawags were rascals, but many really just wanted to help the South. Southerners didn't like the carpetbaggers, either. Northerners who arrived with their belongings in cheap suitcases made of a fabric like carpet were called carpetbaggers. Many Southerners thought those Northerners would stuff their carpetbags with Southern **plunder**. Some carpetbaggers did take advantage of Southerners, but others wanted to help rebuild the South and work for **civil** rights.

For the former slaves, freedom was a mixed blessing. They were left with no property, no jobs, no homes, and were the target of white Southerners' anger over what they had lost. It was difficult to survive.

Shortly before the end of the Civil War, the federal government created the Freedmen's Bureau. African-Americans were supposed to receive small plots of land from the vast areas the Union Army seized during the war. General Sherman had distributed land and army mules to blacks who followed his "march to the sea." Word spread that the federal government intended to give every freed slave "forty acres and a **mule**." Congress did

'Northerners' Carpetbags at the Train Station

give the Freedmen's Bureau control of millions of acres of land for freed slaves, but then President Johnson gave it back to its former white owners. Still, the Bureau did build freedmen schools and colleges across the South.

America's Constitutional **system of checks and balances** gives Congress the power to remove the president from office if he is found guilty of "treason, **bribery**, or other high crimes and **misdemeanors**." The president can only be impeached by a majority of the House of Representatives. Impeachment doesn't remove him from office, it only officially charges him with an **offense**. Then he is **tried**, with the Senate serving as the jury and the chief justice of the United States as judge. The president can only be removed from office when two-thirds of the senators find him guilty.

In February 1868, Andrew Johnson became the first U.S. president to be impeached. Radical Republicans led the move to impeach him after he repeatedly tried to block Reconstruction. No president had ever been impeached before, so no one knew exactly how to conduct the trial. It lasted for more than two months. During the trial, Johnson promised the senators he would no longer oppose Reconstruction, so he was acquitted (declared not guilty of the offense) by only one vote. He would have been removed from office had the vote gone against him.

The country adopted three new Constitutional Amendments shortly after the Civil War:

- The 13th Amendment abolishes slavery.

- The 14th Amendment states:

- All persons born in this country are citizens of the United States and citizens of the states where they live.

- No state may "**deprive** any person of life, liberty, or property, without due process of law." Due process usually gives every person a chance to defend his rights in court.

- No state may deny any person "equal protections of the laws."

- The 15th Amendment forbids state and federal governments from denying or limiting anyone's rights because of race, color or the fact that the person was once a slave.

The Reconstruction Era lasted about 12 years, from 1865 to 1877. During that time, most of the South continued to suffer. Many Southerners claimed Republican state governments were **corrupt**, which was sometimes true. Usually, white Southerners simply did not want African-Americans to be their equals. Some white Southerners refused to do business with or **hire** African-Americans. Some formed secret organizations to scare blacks and friendly whites. The Ku Klux Klan was the worst of these secret organizations. Members of the Klan wore white hoods to hide their faces when they set fire to wooden crosses, burned black churches, schools, houses and even killed innocent black people.

In the early 1870s, some Southern governments did everything they could to deny African-Americans the right to vote. Some states imposed a poll tax, which required a payment to vote. Most blacks couldn't **afford** to pay, so they couldn't vote. By 1877, the federal government was no longer making special efforts to help African-Americans. Most Northerners by this time were willing to let white Southerners govern themselves, even if that meant blacks suffered.

African-Americans would not begin to achieve the equality promised by the 13th, 14th and 15th Amendments for another 75 years.

Ku Klux Klan in their Robes and a Burning Cross

Second Expansion of the United States

By the late 1850s, the outer boundary of the country looked much like it does today. The United States claimed land stretching from the Atlantic Ocean in the east to the Pacific Ocean in the west. As a result of a treaty with Great Britain in 1846, the United States also added more land that became Washington, Oregon and Idaho. In 1848, as a result of the Mexican-American War, the United States gained the territory that became California, Nevada, Utah, Colorado and parts of Arizona and New Mexico. Finally, in 1853, the U.S. bought land from Mexico that now makes up the southern part of Arizona and New Mexico.

In 1853, the United States owned all of the land that it holds today, except for Alaska and Hawaii.

Even though the United States reached "from sea to shining sea," few U.S. citizens lived farther west than Kansas. The West was home to many Native Americans, the people who were here first but were not considered U.S. citizens.

Native Americans considered white settlers—who were pushing west to find new land and new opportunities—a threat to their way of life. As farms, cities and towns were set up throughout the West, conflict often led to violence between the two sides. By the end of the century, the Native Americans considered the westward expansion of the United States a **catastrophe**.

Before Europeans arrived in North America, between 500 and 1,000 different languages were spoken among Native Americans. Major tribes east of the Mississippi River included the Cherokee, Seminole, Delaware, Iroquois, Mohican, Massachusett, Shawnee and Sioux. West of the Mississippi was home to more than 100 major Indian tribes, each with its own customs and beliefs.

In the Southwest desert, Native Americans had lived in highly organized towns and cities for centuries. Spanish conquistadores (conquerors) found them living in towns with "apartment buildings" up to six stories high, made mostly of adobe bricks (a mixture of sand, clay and straw). This was at a time when Europeans almost never had buildings more than three stories high. The Spanish called the tribes "Pueblos," their word for towns. The Pueblos were excellent farmers and very peaceful. They went to war only to defend themselves.

Before the Spanish arrived in the New World, more warlike Indians from the north raided Pueblo villages and stole food. These raiders were called *apaches de nabahu*—"enemies of the cultivated fields" by the Pueblos.

This phrase provided the names for two major tribes: the Apache and the Navajo.

The Apache were **nomadic**, roaming the mountains of the Southwest, hunting and gathering wild foods. They raided other Indians and, later, settlers. The Apache were considered some of the fiercest fighters in the West. The Apache did not settle in towns but lived in the desert, so they had to learn to go long distances without water. In one "game," an Apache boy filled his mouth with water, and then ran four miles—without swallowing a drop.

Originally, the Navajo roamed like the Apache, but the Pueblos taught the Navajo how to grow crops, raise sheep and how to weave beautiful blankets. By the early 1800s, the Navajo were living in settlements across a large area in the present-day states of Arizona and New Mexico.

A Pueblo Village

Tribes with similar customs in fishing, hunting and trading lived along the rocky shores of the Pacific in the Northwest. These Indians used **dugout** canoes and traded along the Columbia River and its **tributaries**, sometimes hundreds of miles from the Pacific shore. The Chinook, a Northwest tribe, became important traders in their villages along the banks of the Columbia. Indians of the Pacific Northwest spoke many different languages, but when different tribes wanted to trade they often used a version of the Chinook language called "Chinook **jargon**."

The Great **Basin** is a mostly barren region that is located east of the Sierra Nevada Mountains and west of the Rocky Mountains. The Great Salt Lake, which is full of water too salty to drink, creates a difficult environment. Not many animals or plants can survive on the dry, rocky soil, but some Native Americans managed to live there. These tribes had to **forage** for long hours every day. Dinner might include antelope, rabbit, bird, snake or rat. However, more frequently, the Indians of the Great Basin ate nuts, seeds, roots and leaves. The state of Utah got its name from two of the major tribes of the Great Basin, the Shoshone and the Ute.

North of the Great Basin is the Northwest **Plateau**—high, mostly level land that extends into Canada. The Plateau tribes hunted and fished. They also gathered berries, nuts, seeds and roots. Among the Plateau Indians, the Nez Perce received their name from the French traders. Since some of the tribes wore rings in their noses, the French called them "pierced nose." The natives called themselves Tsutpeli, "people of the mountains."

From the Rocky Mountains in the west to the Mississippi River in the east, far-reaching grasslands called the Great Plains stretched across the middle of the country. The Great Plains were a vast pasture for enormous herds of wild bison, or buffalo. As many as 60 million buffalo roamed freely across the Great Plains during this time. Most Plains Indians hunted buffalo for food, shelter and tools. The tribes found ways to use every part of the buffalo: from the buffalo's bones and **sinew**, the tribes made tools and weapons—even needles and "thread." The hide (skin) of the buffalo provided clothing and shelter (tent-like homes called teepees).

Before the Spanish brought horses to America, Native Americans hunted on foot, often by **stampeding** buffalo over a cliff. By the 1800s, the Plains Indians were hunting on horseback, but both horse and rider risked being **trampled** by the stampeding herd.

In the eastern part of the Great Plains, many of the tribes also raised crops for part of the year. While the hunting tribes lived in teepees, the farming tribes lived in earth lodges during the growing season. Kansas, Iowa and Missouri got their names from some of these eastern Plains tribes. Whites often called another major tribal group the Sioux, but the Indians

Chinook Trading Route
1790–1840

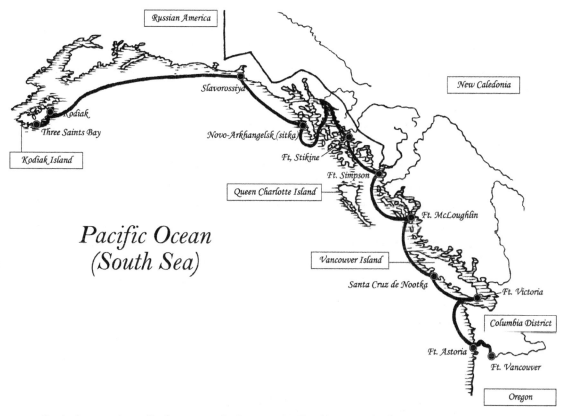

Russian America

Slavorossiya

New Caledonia

Kodiak

Three Saints Bay

Novo-Arkhangelsk (sitka)

Kodiak Island

Ft. Stikine

Ft. Simpson

Queen Charlotte Island

Ft. McLoughlin

*Pacific Ocean
(South Sea)*

Vancouver Island

Santa Cruz de Nootka

Ft. Victoria

Columbia District

Ft. Astoria

Ft. Vancouver

Oregon

called themselves Dakota, or Lakota—"allies" or "the friendly ones." Tribes of the western Great Plains were nomadic, following the herds of buffalo.

In the first half of the 1800s, settlers made slow, unsteady progress West, but in 1848 thousands rushed West. On January 24, 1848 in California, James W. Marshall was building a sawmill by a river for landowner John A. Sutter. When Marshall looked down into the water that ran through the mill, he saw little flakes of dull yellow metal—gold. The news spread quickly throughout the country, and across the sea. Soon thousands headed to California in hopes of striking it rich.

Most of the Gold Rush **miners** reached California in 1849, so they were called "forty-niners." While some forty-niners found gold and became rich, most only found **misery** in crowded mining camps. In these camps, gamblers cheated miners out of their money and shopkeepers charged high prices. The Gold Rush created an urgent need for better ways to move people and supplies out West.

The California territory asked the federal government to build a decent dirt road across the country, and to speed up mail service. Construction began in 1857. A year later, cramped stagecoaches with wooden wheels left Missouri twice a week with passengers and mail on the bumpy three-week trip to San Francisco.

In 1860, a company in Missouri created the Pony Express because three weeks was still too slow for some people. Every 10 miles, all the way to San Francisco, a Pony Express rider would grab a mailbag, leap on a horse, ride at full speed, and then switch without stopping to another horse for the next 10 miles. After 70 miles on seven different horses, the mail was handed to a new rider. This process was repeated until the mail arrived in San Francisco 10 days later. A year and a half later, there was a much faster way to send and receive messages. In October 1861, a coast-to-coast telegraph line was completed. The Pony Express quickly went out of business, because now messages could be sent in seconds instead of days.

By the 1850s, most Americans agreed that the country needed a railroad that **spanned** the continent. No single business could build a transcontinental railroad without government help. So in 1863, Congress gave federal land to private companies and loaned them money to build the railroad. In 1863, the Central Pacific Railroad started laying track in California and headed east.

Pony Express Rider Carrying Mail

In 1864, the Union Pacific Railroad started from Nebraska and headed west. Finally, at Promontory Point, Utah, the Central Pacific track workers linked their track to the Union Pacific track with a golden spike. On May 10, 1869, the United States had its first transcontinental railroad.

The First Transcontinental Railroad

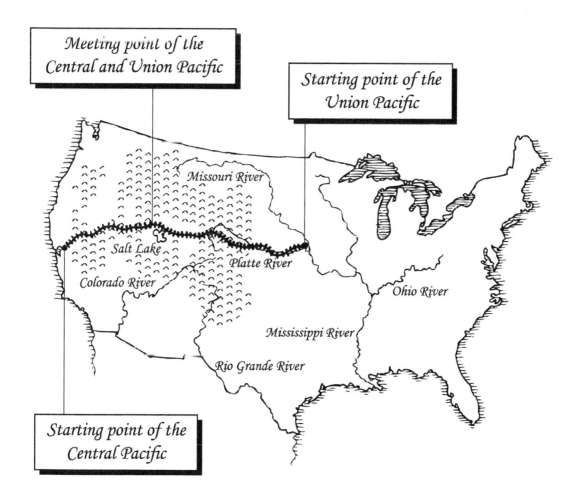

Meeting point of the Central and Union Pacific

Starting point of the Union Pacific

Missouri River

Salt Lake

Platte River

Colorado River

Ohio River

Mississippi River

Rio Grande River

Starting point of the Central Pacific

As railroad use increased, the importance of water travel using canals and steamboats decreased. Railroads made westward expansion possible for businesses as well as for people. Settlers could move West faster and in greater numbers. The railroad companies sold the land they didn't use to the settlers.

In 1862, Congress passed the first Homestead Act. This Act gave 160 acres of free land to any head of a household—even women and former slaves—who would work on the land for at least five years. This free or cheap land created a big demand for rail travel.

John Deere's invention of the steel plow in 1837, Cyrus McCormick's reaper, the harrow in 1869 and barbed wire in 1874 made farming more efficient.

The Wild West

In stories and movies, cowboys are either brave heroes or dangerous **outlaws**. However, in the real West most cowboys usually lived average lives, **tending cattle** and doing chores.

When the Civil War ended, there was a **shortage** of beef in the East while in southern Texas there were millions of freely roaming cattle. Some businessmen decided to gather wild Texas cattle and sell them back East. Since the railroad hadn't reached Texas yet, the cattle would have to walk hundreds of miles to the nearest train station in Kansas. The Long Drive moved 35,000 cattle along the Chisholm Trail to Abilene, Kansas in the first year. Cowboys rode horses alongside the cattle herd to drive (guide or coax) the cattle in the right direction.

Newspapers **exaggerated** reports about the money to be made in cattle ranching. Just as the forty-niners had rushed west to prospect (look) for gold, many people rushed into the cattle business. Wherever there was enough grass for pasture, cattle ranches sprang up.

Starting when Lewis and Clark sent back reports of their 1840 expedition, Americans enjoyed stories about the "Wild West." Some stories about the West stretched the truth and many newspaper writers exaggerated stories to get more people to buy the newspaper. Often when the reports reached the East, stories sometimes had very little truth left in them. A sheriff who arrested a drunken cattle thief might be transformed into a hero who had singlehandedly shot a dozen murderous outlaws. This is how legends about heroes and villains grew and spread.

There were real outlaws, however. Some of the most feared outlaws were Civil War **veterans**. When the war was over, some of these desperate men continued to kill and rob as a way of life.

One of the most **infamous** Western outlaws was Jesse James. He fought in the Civil War with Quantrill's Raiders, a violent group of outlaw Confederates. After the war, Jesse and his brother Frank formed a gang. Legends spread about the brothers during the 25 years they robbed banks and trains. Finally in 1882, Jesse was at home in Missouri with Charles and

Cowboys Watching the Cattle in the Old West

Robert Ford, a couple of younger members of the gang. Jesse was standing on a chair straightening a picture when Robert Ford shot and killed him. Frank James fled but was captured and tried for his crimes. However, he was acquitted.

Another famous outlaw was William Bonney, known as "Billy the Kid." Billy may have killed as many as 12 men before he reached his 18th birthday. Billy and his gang stole cattle and killed anyone who tried to stop them. At the end of 1880, Billy's friend Pat Garrett, a sheriff, trapped Billy's gang and forced Billy to surrender. While waiting to be hanged for murder, Billy killed two jail guards and escaped. Garrett tracked Billy to his hideout and fired a shot into a dark bedroom. At the age of 21, Billy the Kid was dead.

Back in 1840, the U.S. government promised the American Indians they would be allowed to live freely on Western lands. The land west of Missouri and Iowa would remain a "permanent Indian frontier." Most Americans considered the Great Plains a wasteland, so the Indians were welcome to "useless" land. Unfortunately, the Gold Rush, cattle ranching, the spread of railroads and large areas of rich soil combined with the invention of the steel plow proved the West was not useless.

When Native Americans resisted attempts to take their land, the federal government broke its promises. The U.S. government pressured Indian tribes to give up their land in a new promise, or treaty. This new treaty promised that if a tribe would agree to stay within smaller areas, on reservations, then the tribe could live there forever.

Reservations tended to be smaller than the areas the tribes had once lived in, or were located on land that could barely support a few people, let alone whole tribes. Tribes who had been farmers were forced to accept dry, rocky ground. Those who had once roamed over vast areas of the Great Plains hunting for buffalo were forced onto small reservations where the hunting was poor.

The Bureau of Indian Affairs agents were supposed to help Indians adjust to life on the reservations. Sometimes the Bureau did help the Indians and guard their rights under the government treaties, but many others did not understand Indian life. More than a few officials kept the money for the Indians' food and clothing for themselves.

Shortly before the Civil War, events in the West **touched off** a series of wars that **pitted** Indians against settlers and the U.S. Army. In 1859, miners looking for gold in Colorado forced the Cheyenne and Arapaho to leave their homes. Federal officials took the miners' side, and tried to force the tribes to accept a smaller reservation away from the miners. Angry Indians fought back for more than three years. Finally, the weary Indians, led by Chief Black Kettle, surrendered at a federal army **outpost**.

The Indians thought the war was over, but a band of volunteers attacked them at a place called Sand Creek. Chief Black Kettle waved American and white flags as a sign of peace, but the men killed all but a few of the Indians, including babies and children. The federal government didn't apologize for the Sand Creek Massacre until the Cheyenne and Arapaho signed a peace treaty the next year.

In 1874, gold was discovered on the Sioux reservation in the Black Hills (now part of South Dakota). Since the whites now considered the land valuable, the government tried to persuade the Sioux to sell it, or at least **rent** it to gold miners. The Sioux considered the Black Hills **sacred** ground and wouldn't negotiate.

In spring 1876, large numbers of Sioux, Cheyenne and Arapaho warriors joined together to fight the U.S. Army. Sitting Bull and Crazy Horse were two of the Indian leaders. In the army, there was a **brash** young officer, Lieutenant Colonel George Armstrong Custer. Custer ignored orders not to attack, and tried to surprise Sitting Bull and Crazy Horse, who were camped next to a stream called Little Big Horn. Twenty-five hundred Indian warriors quickly surprised and surrounded Custer's 256 army soldiers. Custer and all his men were dead within hours. The Battle of Little Big Horn became famous as "Custer's Last Stand."

The Indians did not win the war in spite of their victory at Little Big Horn. Just months after Custer fell, most of the Indians were forced to surrender. However, Sitting Bull and a small group of followers escaped

Chief Crazy Horse and Lieutenant Colonel Custer

north to Canada. Starvation later forced Sitting Bull's group to return and surrender in 1881.

In 1876, American settlers in the Pacific Northwest claimed Nez Perce land. Rather than fight the U.S. Army, a group led by Chief Joseph fled to Canada. About 750 Native Americans travelled 1,700 miles over just 75 days, fighting four major battles with the U.S. Army along the way. As Chief Joseph and his people rested just 30 miles from the Canadian border, the U.S. Army surprised them. The 87 remaining warriors fought bravely for five days before they finally surrendered. Chief Joseph and the Nez Perce were scattered to reservations all over the West.

Many Americans wanted to help the Indians. Most well-meaning Americans thought helping the Indians meant **assimilating** them, making them be like Americans. In reality, that meant destroying their cultures. In 1879, the Carlisle Indian School opened in Pennsylvania. Native American children were taken from their families on Western reservations and sent across the country for mechanical and agricultural training and lessons in good citizenship. While many Native Americans understood the need for education, they didn't trust the new schools, which often taught Native American children to reject their people's ways. The children were not allowed to wear their tribal clothes, speak their own languages or practice tribal customs.

Indian tribes traditionally believed no single person owned a piece of land—land belonged to all the members of the tribe. In contrast, Americans believe that individuals owned land. In the 1880s, many white Americans believed that private land ownership would help the Indians. This was another example of thinking that Indians should give up their ways and think like Americans. Most Indians were puzzled by this idea, but in 1887 Congress passed the Dawes Severalty Act. Under this law, the head of each Indian household would be given 160 acres on the reservation. Once every family had its "**allotment**," any remaining land could be sold.

Many people believed that this law would simply allow Americans to take over more Indian land, and they were right. As soon as an individual Indian owned the land, he could sell it. Since most Indians were poor, they sold their land to white people to be able to buy necessities. The system eventually caused the Indians to lose most of their lands, and they were left with nothing. Finally, in 1934, Congress passed a law to stop the **breakup** of the reservations.

In 1867, the United States bought Alaska from Russia. Many Americans called it a **folly** to buy such a cold land. Exploration, however, eventually revealed a land full of forests, minerals, oil and gold. The United States also

The United States
1920

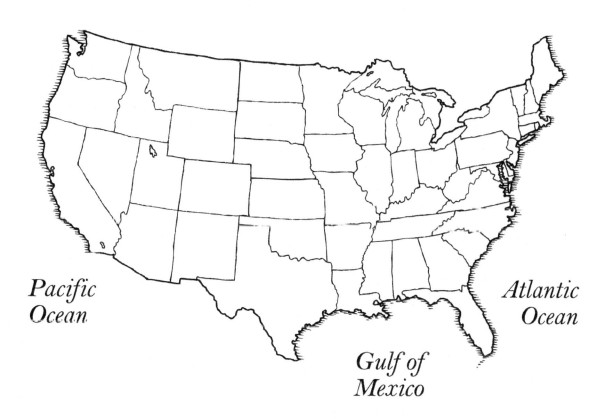

Pacific
Ocean

Atlantic
Ocean

Gulf of
Mexico

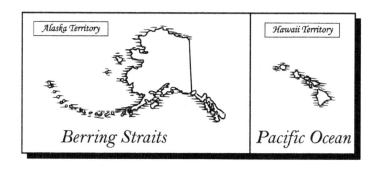

Alaska Territory

Berring Straits

Hawaii Territory

Pacific Ocean

took over the Midway Islands during this time, but no one realized their future importance in 1867.

In 1898, The Republic of Hawaii, which had its own government and ruler, was taken over as an American territory. American businessmen who had investments in the sugar fields there paid for a short conflict to take over the island chain.

During this period of U.S. expansion, the United States celebrated its' centennial (1876), with a big exposition in Philadelphia. Many modern inventions were on display, as well as works of art, buildings and more. Following the successful exposition, the French people wanted to give a gift to the U.S. to commemorate the American Revolution and to honor President Lincoln's efforts. The Statue of Liberty was built and sent to the U.S. in 1885. It was placed on Liberty Island in New York harbor in 1886. The statue was designed to be a symbol of enlightenment and freedom, but to the immigrants who came to America it was a welcome symbol of hope and opportunity. Emma Lazarus wrote the poem that is attached at the base of the statue (see Appendix F).

Industry and invention **boomed** between the Civil War and the early 20th century. Between 1860 and 1900, the United States Patent Office issued patents for more than a half million inventions. A patent is a special right awarded to an inventor who proves that his invention is both new and useful. When the patent is awarded, no one may use, make or sell the invention without the inventor's permission. A patent holder may become rich if enough people are willing to pay for the invention.

Thomas Edison patented more than 1,000 devices and processes. The phonograph, motion pictures (movies) and the electric lamp are three of his most famous inventions. Edison did not actually invent the electric lamp, but he solved problems and improved upon earlier versions, which is a common practice of many inventors. Before Edison, electric light was expensive, but he and his team of researchers developed a better electric light and a system to cheaply generate electricity. Because of Edison's inventions, cities could replace their dim gaslights with bright electric streetlights.

Alexander Graham Bell was working on new type of telegraph. During an experiment, Bell was surprised when his machine transmitted the sound of human speech from another room. With electrical engineer Thomas Watson, Bell developed his accidental discovery into the first working telephone.

George Washington Carver, who was born a slave during the Civil War, was an important African-American scientist and inventor. Most blacks during Carver's time received little or no schooling, but Carver managed

Inventions

Many inventions were developed and/or perfected between 1780-1870. Below is only a partial list. Not all were invented by Americans but many were. Look at the list and decide what area of society benefited the most the invention (industry, transportation, home, agriculture).

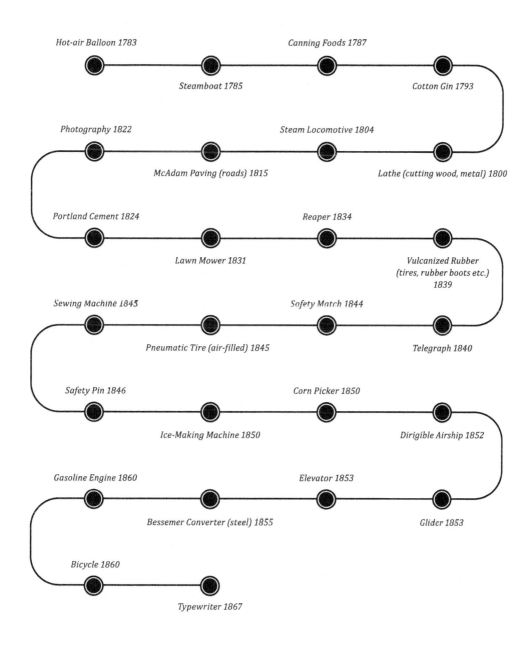

Hot-air Balloon 1783

Canning Foods 1787

Steamboat 1785

Cotton Gin 1793

Photography 1822

Steam Locomotive 1804

McAdam Paving (roads) 1815

Lathe (cutting wood, metal) 1800

Portland Cement 1824

Reaper 1834

Lawn Mower 1831

Vulcanized Rubber (tires, rubber boots etc.) 1839

Sewing Machine 1845

Safety Match 1844

Pneumatic Tire (air-filled) 1845

Telegraph 1840

Safety Pin 1846

Corn Picker 1850

Ice-Making Machine 1850

Dirigible Airship 1852

Gasoline Engine 1860

Elevator 1853

Bessemer Converter (steel) 1855

Glider 1853

Bicycle 1860

Typewriter 1867

to earn an advanced college degree in botany, the study of plants. He then taught botany and modern farming techniques to other African-Americans in Alabama.

Carver discovered that the soil in Alabama and other parts of the South had been ruined by years of growing only cotton. Carver told Southern farmers that, in addition to cotton, they must grow plants like peanuts and sweet potatoes, which put **nutrients** back into to the soil. Carver's advice worked, but farmers then produced more peanuts and sweet potatoes than people would buy. Carver developed hundreds of products in the lab that could be made from peanuts and sweet potatoes, including plastics, dyes, medicines, flour, peanut butter, powdered milk and fertilizer.

One new idea, adopted in 1883, divided the world into 24 time zones, one for each hour of the day. Establishing standard times made train travel easier. Before then, noon occurred at a different time of day at every stop, based on the location of the sun in the sky. It could be 12:15 in one town when it was 12:37 in the next town. This was not a problem before trains, but trains need to run on standard schedules. Time zones were established at an international meeting in 1884. Congress made time zones the national standard in 1918.

Industrialization in the United States

After the Civil War, many Americans moved from living and working on farms to living in cities and working in factories. Both progress and problems resulted from these new industries. The country grew wealthy, but not everyone shared in the wealth. A huge gap existed between the workers and those who owned the industries. The owners were called "capitalists."

Capital is money, and capitalists put their money in to industries for profit. Many businesses and industries, like railroads, required a great deal of capital. To get enough capital, several capitalists would combine their money to form a corporation. When people invested money in the corporation, they would own a share of the corporation, and would receive a share of the profits.

Andrew Carnegie was a tremendously rich capitalist, who owned many factories that made steel. With the growth of railroads, which required thousands of miles of steel track, the steel industry in America was booming. When the Civil War was over, Carnegie saw the need for more steel, so he invested in the iron and steel industry in Pittsburgh, Pennsylvania.

Carnegie's success in the steel business demonstrates how some capitalists built powerful monopolies. A monopoly is exclusive control over an industry or economic market. Carnegie monopolized the steel industry by building steel **mills** that produced steel faster. Carnegie bought iron **ore** mines and coal mines to ensure a steady supply of **raw materials**. Carnegie also bought railroads and shipping companies to transport iron and coal from the mines to the mills. Since Carnegie controlled everything needed to make steel, his company sold steel at lower prices. Other companies could not match his prices and he soon drove the other steel companies out of business. Then he controlled most of the steel business and could charge what he wanted.

A Steel Mill in the Northeast

Capitalists in other businesses also created huge monopolies, eventually called trusts. John D. Rockefeller's Standard Oil Co. Inc. (later the Standard Oil trust) took over oil processing plants, called "refineries." John Pierpont "J.P." Morgan gained a monopoly over the country's system of banks. The railroads became a monopoly controlled by Cornelius Vanderbilt. Vanderbilt's methods were **ruthless**, but he made the railroads more efficient.

By 1900, a small group of powerful trusts dominated America's most important industries, including copper, sugar, rubber, leather, farm machinery and telephones. Carnegie, Rockefeller, Morgan and others became extremely wealthy. Some capitalists were also philanthropists. They devoted part of their wealth to helping others. Some donated to charity, or built libraries, museums and colleges.

As machinery changed America's industries, it also changed the lives of the workers—but not always for the better. Machines now did many of the jobs once performed by human hands. Workers only took care of the machines and did whatever work the machines could not do. To keep the machines running, men, women and children worked 10-12 hours per day, six days a week.

Despite the millions of dollars in profits that factory owners made, factory workers earned very little. Whole families often had to live in a single room with no running water. The factory machines usually had no safety devices to protect workers from injury. Many workers joined labor unions to improve working conditions. Union workers demanded better pay and better working conditions. Workers would go on strike (stop working) if the demands were not met. If a large group of workers went on strike, they could **disrupt** or even shut down an entire company, which forced owners to listen to the workers.

Corporations sometimes granted some of the workers' demands, but often the owners responded with violence. In 1892, at one of Carnegie's steel mills in Homestead, Pennsylvania, workers went on strike because he reduced their already-low pay by almost 20 percent. The company didn't want to meet the workers' demands, so they locked them out and hired new workers. The union workers lost their jobs.

Still, American industry made this country attractive to poor immigrants looking for a better life. People around the world called the United States "the land of opportunity." Between 1850 and 1930, 35 million people immigrated to the United States—the greatest movement of people in the history of the world. Immigrants coming from Europe entered through Ellis Island in Upper New York Bay and immigrants coming from Asia entered through Angel Island in San Francisco.

Before the Civil War, most immigrants came from northern and western Europe. After the Civil War, more immigrants arrived from southern and eastern Europe. Eager for work, immigrants made important contributions to America. Alexander Graham Bell and Andrew Carnegie were both from Scotland. Immigrant workers from China and Ireland did much of the **grueling** work building the transcontinental railroads.

Some immigrants pushed West, while others stayed in eastern cities where they could remain close to other immigrants from the old country. In these cities, neighborhoods like Little Italy or Chinatown developed.

Labor Unions on Strike and the Lockout

Immigrants crowded into rundown **tenements,** where newcomers could find help and comfort from fellow countrymen.

The United States was a powerful, industrialized nation. Americans generally enjoyed greater civil liberties than any other people on earth. Free public education, while only a dream in most parts of the world, was a reality in the United States. America still faced problems in transforming itself from a mainly agricultural country, relying on slavery in the South, to an industrialized nation.

With cities and factories came difficult conditions for workers and the poor. Reformers like Dorothea Dix and Horace Mann worked to improve conditions in America in the early 1860s. Later, toward the end of the 19th century, new reformers rose to the challenges that the **urban** poor, African-Americans, women and farmers had to **confront**.

Farmers were in trouble after the Civil War. The availability of new farmland and modern farm machinery forced farmers to reduce crop prices. At the same time, they were charged high railroad prices to get their crops to market. The farmers formed the People's Party, or Populists, in 1892, to challenge the Democratic and Republican parties. Populists saw the country moving away from Thomas Jefferson's vision of a land of independent farmers and toward domination by big corporations and industries. In the 1896 presidential election, Democrat William Jennings Bryan favored many Populist ideas, but Republican William McKinley, supported by big business, won the election. This defeat marked the end of the Populists as a national party.

Social Change

In many of America's cities, poor people lived in **filthy slums**. Jane Addams of Cedarville, Illinois, was not poor, or from a big city, but she was determined to help the less fortunate. Like many young women from **well-off** families in the late 1800s, Addams toured Europe with a friend. However, the women did not visit museums and cathedrals. They went to factories and slums. Reformers who lived among the poor in London **settlement houses** inspired Addams to open Hull House in Chicago, Illinois in 1889. The community center provided food and shelter, medical services, music and art to the poor. Hull House also provided childcare for working mothers, a hot meal for the hungry and help finding a job for the unemployed.

Addams' "experiment" challenged the generally accepted beliefs that life was a matter of "survival of the fittest"—only the strong can and should get ahead. Addams believed it was better to feed the hungry and care for the sick, and help the young and old.

Addams also opposed widespread **prejudice** against new immigrants. Americans who were children or grandchildren of immigrants looked upon the new immigrants as "foreigners." Addams saw prejudice make children, especially from poor **backgrounds**, ashamed of their parents and their heritage. She encouraged immigrant children to draw strength from their pasts. She reminded them that Abraham Lincoln never denied his humble origins. Reformers in other American cities began to **emulate** Addams and Hull House.

Americans read more stories in newspapers and magazines about corrupt practices in business and government, and about the suffering of poor people in big cities. The journalists who wrote these true stories were called "muckrakers." They raked (scraped) through the muck—the unpleasant, dirty side—of American life, to encourage the public to clean up corruption and stop the suffering. Jacob Riis, a Danish immigrant who settled in New York City. was one of the first muckrakers. In 1890, Riis described life in New York's crowded, filthy slums in a book, *How the Other Half Lives*. It **condemned** New York slums like Murderer's Alley and Misery Row. Appalling photographs illustrated Riis's vivid words. When readers saw the terrible conditions, many joined Riis in his demand for better housing, better living conditions and decent schools for the poor.

African-Americans were still denied equal opportunities to improve themselves in America. Booker T. Washington believed education was essential to a better life for African-Americans. He helped establish the Tuskegee Normal and Industrial Institute in Alabama in 1881. Under Washington's leadership, Tuskegee University grew to become an important black education center, preparing its students to become teachers and skilled tradesmen.

As a result of George Washington Carver joining the faculty, Tuskegee Institute

The First Building of the Tuskegee Institute

began teaching modern farming techniques. Washington told blacks that they must first raise their economic status, before they could expect to win social and political equality. He also said they must be patient.

African-American reformer W.E.B. Du Bois disagreed. Washington asked for quiet patience, but Du Bois urged African-Americans to insist loudly upon the equal rights promised in the 14th Amendment. Du Bois and other well-educated blacks met at Niagara Falls, Canada in 1905 to form a civil rights group called the Niagara Movement. Members of the Niagara Movement had joined white reformers in 1909 to create the National Association for the Advancement of Colored People, now called the NAACP. Du Bois became the first editor of the NAACP publication called *The Crisis*. The NAACP was a leading organization in the fight for racial equality throughout the 20th century.

During Reconstruction, African-Americans in the South gained rights and **privileges** but, by the late 1800s, many white Southerners increasingly ignored the black Americans' civil rights. Some southern states imposed "**Jim Crow**" laws, ("Jim Crow" was insulting slang for African-Americans). Some individuals joined groups like the Ku Klux Klan, or joined a mob to lynch black Americans (to hang them without a trial or any evidence that they had done anything illegal). Race-based lynching continued from the late 19th century into the early 20th century.

In the late 1800s, the United States became involved in the affairs of three Spanish colonies: Cuba, Puerto Rico and the Philippine Islands. Cuba was Spain's most important colony in the Western **Hemisphere**, but Cuba shipped most of its valuable sugar and tobacco to the United States, rather than to Spain. The United States tried several times to buy Cuba from Spain in the 1800s. Spain refused to sell the island, but the countries remained allies. After the American Civil War, the Cubans began to fight Spain in its own war of independence. By the end of 1895, Cuban patriots were winning the war.

Americans received news of the fighting in Cuba through the newspapers. Some "yellow journalists" stretched the truth, or even made up wild stories, to sell more newspapers. They made the war in Cuba front-page news by exaggerating the already cruel treatment of the Cubans by the Spanish.

Largely because of these inaccurate reports, many Americans urged the U.S. government to declare war against Spain. Many Americans favored Cuban **revolutionaries**, but the U.S. government refused to get directly involved. Fighting had reached the Cuban capital of Havana by early 1898. Many Spaniards urged their government to free Cuba. The U.S. Navy sent the battleship USS Maine to Havana harbor, to help Americans there, but not to attack. Then on February 15, 1898, an explosion on the Maine killed

260 Americans and the ship sank. Today, studies say the explosion was an accident, but in 1898 yellow journalists blamed Spain. Many Americans demanded America go to war to free Cuba and avenge the deaths on the Maine.

Congress declared war on Spain on April 25, 1898. The United States had an immediate advantage over Spain: its larger and more modern Navy. U.S. Navy ships were ordered to attack Spanish ships wherever they found them. On May 1, 1898, the first battle occurred far from Cuba. American Navy ships sailed into Manila Bay in the Philippines. Spanish guns fired on the American ships, but the Americans quickly sank or **disabled** the Spanish ships.

Meanwhile back in Cuba, the Spanish navy was trapped. Most Spanish warships had taken cover in the harbor of Santiago. The American Navy **blockaded** the harbor and landed 18,000 American troops on the Cuban coast. Americans attacked Spanish outposts near Santiago. One of the Americans, Theodore Roosevelt and his regiment of volunteers, the Rough Riders, led a successful charge up San Juan Hill.

While soldiers were killed or wounded on both sides, by July 1, Americans controlled the hills overlooking Santiago. American guns

The Naval Blockade of Havana's Harbor in Cuba

destroyed nearly all of the Spanish fleet as it tried to escape. By August 12, 1898, the Spanish-American War was over.

The peace treaty that ended the Spanish-American War gave the United States an overseas empire. It was similar to the empire of Great Britain, except that the United States called its new lands territories, rather than colonies. Spain gave up Cuba, and also gave the United States control of Puerto Rico and Guam, a Mariana island in the Pacific. (Puerto Rico and Guam are still U.S. territories.) Spain also sold the Philippines to the United States for $20 million.

Many Americans believed that establishing an empire **violated** the principles of the *Declaration of Independence*. There was so much opposition to an **imperial** America that, when the peace treaty with Spain went before Congress for approval, it passed by only one vote.

Cuba was not a United States territory, but American troops **occupied** and controlled Cuba for two years after the peace treaty was signed. In 1901, the United States required Cuba to give the United States the right to decide whether Cubans had created a "government adequate for the protection of life, property and individual liberty." The United States used this law several times in the early 20th century to send troops to Cuba to protect American business interests there.

The Americans had helped the Filipinos declare their independence from Spain, and then made the Philippines an American territory. After the Spanish-American War ended, the Filipino rebels continue to fight the U.S. for two more years. The rebels finally surrendered after the Americans captured their leader in 1901. The Philippines finally gained their independence from the U.S. in 1946.

Theodore Roosevelt, the 26th president of the United States, was popularly known as "Teddy," and the teddy bear was named after him. Roosevelt was not elected president. He was President William McKinley's vice president. When McKinley was **assassinated** at the beginning of his term, Roosevelt became president.

Roosevelt was also an active reformer and when the government passed laws to reform the **brutal** practices of American business trusts, he became known as a "trust-buster." He was not opposed to big business, but wanted government to have the power to keep it honest. Businessmen were shocked because they were not used to government telling them how to run their businesses. Before the government passed the Meat Inspection Act of 1906, you never knew what you might be eating, or whether it would make you sick.

Roosevelt was a great sportsman who loved the outdoors. Americans were destroying the wilderness with logging and mining. He stopped this

United States
Imperialism
1857-1906

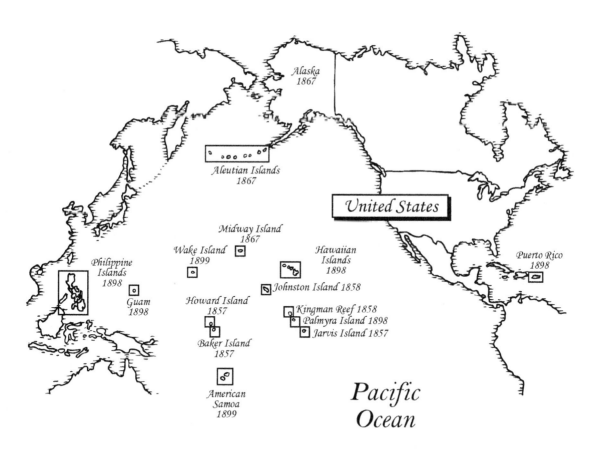

Alaska
1867

Aleutian Islands
1867

United States

Midway Island
1867

Wake Island
1899

Hawaiian
Islands
1898

Puerto Rico
1898

Philippine
Islands
1898

Johnston Island 1858

Guam
1898

Howard Island
1857

Kingman Reef 1858
Palmyra Island 1898
Jarvis Island 1857

Baker Island
1857

American
Samoa
1899

*Pacific
Ocean*

destruction by urging Congress to create a conservation program to limit damage to the American natural **resources** and protect forests. He doubled the number of national parks, and created the park system that exists today.

Before Roosevelt became president, some Americans wanted a Central American canal to connect the Pacific Ocean to the Atlantic Ocean. The United States paid Panama $10 million and agreed to pay $250,000 in rent per year. The United States began construction of the canal in 1904, and finished it in 1914.

The Panama Canal

Moving Into the World
1910-1950

World Wars

The world began to consider the United States a powerful nation after its easy victory over Spain. It soon became a central player in world events.

In 1914, a war broke out in Europe that involved so many nations that it was called the Great War, or the World War. Sadly, it later had to be called the First World War, or World War I. The conflict began in Europe. The Allies were on one side, led by France, Great Britain, Russia and Austria-Hungary. On the other side were the Central Powers, led by Germany. Three bloody years later, in 1917, the United States joined the Allies. That would turn out to be one of the most important decisions in United States history.

From then on, the United States became more involved in the affairs of foreign countries. After World War I, America's actions would affect people all over the globe, and its responsibilities would weigh heavily on Americans.

More soldiers died in World War I than in any previous war, at home or abroad. The war was bloodier and more destructive than other wars because soldiers had new weapons. For the first time, tanks and airplanes were used in battle. Submarines were deadly new weapons at sea. Huge cannons hurled bigger, more explosive shells farther than ever before. In some battles, a terrible new weapon, poison gas, was used and thousands of soldiers were blinded, wounded or killed. The greatest loss of life, however, was caused by the new machine gun. In earlier wars, even in the Civil War (the bloodiest war in history before World War I) a soldier could only fire one shot at a time with a rifle. However, in World War I, a single soldier with one machine gun could fire more than 400 bullets a minute, and kill dozens, or even hundreds, of enemy soldiers.

Since both sides had machine guns, neither army had an advantage. The war soon stalled, with soldiers on each side stuck in protective ditches called trenches. Life in the trenches was harsh, wet and dirty. The soldiers were bitten by fleas and lice, rats stole their food and the trenches filled with water and mud when it rained. When one side tried to attack the other side's soldiers in the trenches, the attackers were **mowed down** by enemy machine guns as they charged across the "no man's land" between the two sides.

The brutality of the conflict was horrifying to Americans. Until 1917, most Americans agreed the U.S. should remain neutral—not take a side. The Americans eventually became sympathetic to the Allies. Englishmen and Americans spoke the same language, and a number of basic American ideas and institutions came from England. Americans also sympathized with France, where the war was being fought, because the French had helped them win the Revolutionary War. In the end, however, two Germans actions angered Americans enough to send them to war.

American Troops in the Trenches Fighting in World War I

When World War I began, the British had the most powerful navy on earth. It blockaded the German coast to prevent ships from carrying supplies to Germany. The much smaller German navy could not break the blockade, so it set up its own blockade around England—an underwater blockade. While the Germans had fewer surface ships than the British, they had submarines, or as the English called them, "U-boats," from the German word for "undersea boat." Germany ordered its U-boats to sink any ship that tried to supply England and warned that passengers would be travelling at their own risk on these ships.

In May 1915, the British passenger ship Lusitania steamed from New York City toward England. Suddenly, the captain heard a watch officer shout, "**Torpedo** coming!" Before the captain could react, a U-boat torpedo exploded in the center of the ship. The Lusitania sank in less than 20 minutes. It was so quick that many passengers had no time to get into lifeboats. More than 1,000 people, including 128 Americans, were killed.

Americans were outraged. America complained to Germany, but the Germans replied that the people on the Lusitania had been warned. They also claimed that the ship had been carrying arms for the Allies. To avoid killing more civilians, the Germans gave new, stricter orders to their U-boat captains. Still, Americans remembered the Lusitania.

The Sinking of the Lusitania

American anger **simmered** for more than a year. It boiled over in early 1917, when Germany announced that U-boats would sink *any* ship sailing toward England, not just supply ships. Then, Germany sent a telegram to a German diplomat in Mexico, offering a secret deal. If Mexico joined the Central Powers, Germany would help Mexico retake the territories it lost in the Mexican-American War. These territories had become the states of Arizona, New Mexico and Texas. British spies warned the U.S. government about the offer.

Until now, President Woodrow Wilson had kept the United States out of the war. Even the sinking of the Lusitania did not change his mind. The deal offered in the telegram changed his mind. Wilson asked Congress to declare war on Germany in April 1917. In his speech, he said that the world must be made safe for democracy. Within days, America was at war. About 2 million men volunteered to join the military and almost 3 million more were drafted. It would be months before American soldiers could be trained and arrive in Europe to fight.

One of the Allies, Russia, was a huge and powerful country, but most of the people were poor and **uneducated**. A **czar**, whose undemocratic government denied many basic human rights to the Russian people, ruled Russia. The war made the poor Russian people even poorer. Many were starving. In 1917, the people **overthrew** the czar in the Russian Revolution. The czar, his wife and their children were killed.

It appeared at first that Russia might become a democracy, but a group called the Bolsheviks took over within eight months. They proved to be even more tyrannical than the czar. Bolsheviks followed Karl Marx, whose ideas helped create **communism**. Marx believed it was wrong that a few people were rich and powerful, and all the rest were poor. He believed that workers all over the world would unite to overthrow the rich ruling class. Finally, he thought, everyone would be equal.

In October 1917, the Bolsheviks, under the leadership of the revolutionary Vladimir Lenin and with the help of poor workers, took over Russia. The hungry and war-weary Russian people were attracted by Lenin's promise of "Peace, Land and Bread." Under Lenin, the Bolshevik Party won a bloody civil war that killed millions of Russians. The party changed its name to the Communist Party, and renamed the country the Soviet Union. A "soviet" was a council of workers that was supposed to allow the people to participate in government. The communists claimed to rule in the name of the majority of Russians—workers and **peasants**. In fact, communists were a small minority who kept the power for themselves.

Lenin's government deserted the Allies and signed a peace treaty with Germany. This gave Germany a huge advantage and Germany appeared to be winning the war. German troops pushed deep into France, marching to within 50 miles of Paris, the French capital.

When the American troops arrived in France in late 1917, Col. Charles Stanton declared, "Lafayette, we are here" to return Lafayette's great favor. The arrival of American troops helped to **turn the tide** of the war. The Allies were tired, but Americans were fresh from home and fought fiercely against the weary Germans. The Americans' arrival also raised the spirits of French and British troops. Together, the Allies pushed the Germans back toward the French border. Germany realized that it would lose, and offered to make peace with the Allies. The shooting stopped in November 1918.

Representatives from 27 countries met near Paris at the Palace of Versailles. On June 28, 1919, they signed the Treaty of Versailles. This treaty forced the Germans to say that they started the war. It seized German colonies and forced Germany to pay billions of dollars in fines to the Allies. The treaty left the Germans angry. They didn't really believe they were to blame for the war.

The treaty also created the League of Nations. It was to be a great assembly in which all nations could meet and settle conflicts peacefully. Those who approved the creation of the League of Nations hoped it would make the Great War "the war to end all wars." President Wilson came up with the idea for the League of Nations, but he could not convince Americans that the U.S should join it.

Many Americans thought the United States should be able to do what it wanted to do, without asking permission from other nations, so the Senate refused to approve the Treaty of Versailles. President Wilson was heartbroken at the decision. The United States signed a separate treaty with Germany in 1921, and became only an observer at League meetings.

Refusing to join the League of Nations was only one sign of increasing **"isolationism"** in America. Isolationists wanted the United States to stay out of issues in the rest of the world.

After World War I, many Americans feared there would be a flood of immigrants from the war-torn countries of Europe. Congress severely limited the number of immigrants to the U.S. The new laws were intended to restrict the arrival of people whose religious and political ideas were different from most Americans. Many people believed that only Protestants of Northern European descent were "true" or "pure" Americans. Many Americans were especially suspicious of immigrants from southern and eastern Europe, who were often Catholic or Jewish. Ku Klux Klan membership and activity surged in the 1920s, and now they attacked Catholics and Jews as well as blacks.

The 1920s was a difficult decade for minorities, but it was also a time of widespread **prosperity** and technological progress. Many people had more money to spend, and manufacturers produced more products for them to buy. Most American homes had electricity, so Americans enjoyed products that made life more comfortable—new machines like the vacuum cleaner, the washing machine, gas and electric stoves and the refrigerator.

The thing that really changed American life was the automobile. Gasoline-powered automobiles were first sold in the 1890s, but were so expensive that only the wealthy could afford them. Then in 1908, American businessman Henry Ford began to make a car called the Model T. The Model T wasn't very pretty. Legend says Ford told buyers they could have it "painted any color ... so long as it is black." Still, it was well built, and cheap enough for the average person to buy. It became the most popular automobile in America at that time.

Ford had **figured out** that he could make cars less expensively on an assembly line. Rather than one worker assembling a whole vehicle, many workers added one piece at a time as the car moved along in front of them. The assembly line allowed Ford to produce cars more quickly and sell them more cheaply.

Mass automobile ownership changed life in America forever. It allowed isolated rural families to travel more easily to the city, and allowed women

One of the First American Automobiles

and young people to become more independent. Americans liked the speed, convenience and freedom of an automobile. This new form of transportation was so popular that, by the end of the 1920s, the auto industry employed more workers than any other industry in the United States. The automobile industry was a symbol of America's successful free enterprise system.

Airplanes were still small and **fragile** in the 1920s, and it took courage to fly them, especially over long distances. In 1927, a young American named Charles Lindbergh astonished the world by flying thousands of miles alone over the stormy north Atlantic Ocean, from New York City to Paris, France. The flight took 33 hours with no sleep. By the end of the flight, Lindbergh was so sleepy that he had to hold his eyelids open with his fingers. He flew through a thick fog that kept him from seeing where he was going and he almost crashed into the ocean several times. Lindbergh was nicknamed "Lucky Lindy," and was cheered as an American hero. His plane, the Spirit of St. Louis, became the most famous aircraft in the world.

In the decade after Lindbergh's amazing achievement, pilot Amelia Earhart became as famous as Lindbergh. In 1932, she became the first person to repeat this remarkable action, and the first woman to fly solo across the Atlantic. She also became the first person to fly solo from California to Hawaii. Finally, in 1937, Earhart tried another first—flying all the way around the world.

She and her navigator started in California, heading east. She flew to Florida, then down to South America and across the Atlantic to Africa. Her route took her across the Middle East, and then to India, Southeast Asia and Australia. Admirers cheered her everywhere she landed for rest and fuel. Six weeks later, however, the world mourned after her plane disappeared in the South Pacific. Earhart and her navigator flew more than three-quarters of the way around the world before they disappeared. Earhart and her plane were never found.

New inventions gave Americans new ways to spend their leisure time. Families gathered nightly around their radios in the 1920s, to listen to news and music, comedy shows, religious broadcasts, mysteries and programs for children. People also started going to motion pictures (movies). Movies in the 1920s were filmed in black and white. Before 1927, they were also silent. Actors appeared to speak on the screen, followed by words written on small signs. Musicians often played dramatic piano or organ music in the theater.

Movies showed audiences Westerns (stories about the Wild West), love stories, adventures in **exotic** lands and stories based on the Bible. Comedies, however, were the favorite. Charlie Chaplin starred in, and often wrote and directed, a series of comedies starring a character called "The Little Tramp." This character was a poor, shy, little man who got into and out of trouble. The character was recognized all over the world by his square mustache, round bowler hat, baggy pants, big shoes and the cane he swung as he walked a funny little **strut**.

The 1920s are called the "Roaring Twenties" because they were exciting, fast-paced times. Young people began to rebel against the strict rules that older Americans had lived by. Many decided to enjoy life, rather than work hard. They were tired of all the **sacrifices** they made during World War I.

Americans also spent a lot of money and drank a lot of alcohol, even though liquor was illegal. For years "temperance" advocates had attacked the use of alcohol. In 1919, Congress passed the 18th Amendment, which **prohibited** the making and selling of beer, wine and alcohol. Prohibition lasted from 1920 to 1933, when Americans **ratified** the 21st Amendment to repeal the 18th Amendment.

Although Prohibition reduced the number of Americans who drank alcohol, many drank in secret. Making

Charlie Chaplin as "The Little Tramp"

liquor illegal, however, made it more attractive to many people, who started going to illegal bars called "speakeasies." **Bootleggers** sold the alcohol to the speakeasies. The word "bootlegger" comes from the old **smuggler's** trick of hiding a bottle inside the leg of a boot. **Gangsters** ran many of the speakeasies, so Prohibition actually led to the development of **organized crime**.

Many speakeasy customers were young women. Women had only won the vote in 1920, with passage of the 19th Amendment. They had not been allowed to drink in public, and most bars didn't allow women. That was just one of the ways that women broke the old rules in the 1920s. The fun-loving, carefree young women who visited the speakeasies were called "flappers," after the odd new dances that became popular to fast, jazzy music. Flappers not only drank, they smoked cigarettes, wore makeup and dresses that only reached their knees. Before World War I, dresses covered women's legs.

New industries developed after the war. Factories needed workers, but immigration restrictions meant fewer people arrived from Europe to work there. So, jobs and the possibility of a better life attracted many African-Americans to leave their Southern farms and head north to the cities. Blacks hoped to encounter less racial prejudice in the North. Many African-Americans moved to Chicago and New York City. The New York City black population in 1930 was six times what it was in 1920. It grew from about 50,000 to more than 300,000. Many transplanted African-Americans made their homes in a New York City neighborhood called Harlem. They found an independence and pride in their traditions there and made Harlem a great center of African-American culture.

This powerful idea of black pride would influence a new generation of African-American artists to start the "Harlem Renaissance," a period during which black artists, writers and scholars were very creative. The Harlem Renaissance marked the rise of "the New Negro," the African-American who, according to one historian, was "black and proud, politically assertive and economically independent, creative and disciplined." (Negro was commonly used during this time to refer to African-Americans, but is not appropriate now.)

A leading Harlem Renaissance figure was poet Langston Hughes, who said black artists and writers should make themselves happy with their work, not attempt to please whites. Some of Hughes' poems spoke of dreams of freedom and equality, others celebrated the energy of life in black communities like Harlem. Many poems expressed ideas and feelings that apply to all people. Much of his poetry reflected black culture, imitating

A Flapper Having a Drink in a Speakeasy

the rhythm of popular African-American forms of music, especially jazz and blues.

At the same time, fundamentalism, the idea that all knowledge comes from the Bible, not science, was on the rise. Tennessee made it illegal to teach Charles Darwin's theory of evolution, but a young Tennessee teacher, John T. Scopes, ignored the law and taught evolution in his biology class. In 1925, Scopes was tried in Tennessee for teaching evolution, which said people evolved from lower animals, like apes. The idea of evolution opposed "creationism," the belief that the world was created by God in seven days, just as it was described in the Bible. William Jennings Bryan **prosecuted** Scopes in the infamous "Monkey Trial," while Clarence Darrow defended him. Scopes lost the first trial and had to **pay a fine**, but the Tennessee Supreme Court later overturned that fine.

Tennessee's anti-evolution law did not change until 1967. Now Tennessee is involved in another legal battle—this time to allow the schools to teach creationism along with evolution.

The Theory of Evolution Argued at the Scopes Trial

The Depression Years

Most Americans lived better during the 1920s, but the 1930s were just the opposite. That decade was a time of great **poverty**. Millions of Americans lost their jobs and homes, and struggled to feed their families. This time was known as the "Great Depression."

Many historians still debate over what caused the Depression, but most agree that American industry grew too rapidly during the 1920s. More things were produced than people could buy. The factories had to slow production and the workers lost their jobs. People had also been spending too much money. They borrowed money to pay for whatever they wanted, or paid "on installment," a little bit at a time—which put them further and further in **debt**. When they lost their jobs, they couldn't pay their debts.

Many people had also been **reckless** with investments, especially in the stock market. When you buy a stock (a share in a company), you own a little piece of the company. Buying stock in a company gives the company money to grow. When the company makes a profit, you are entitled to a portion, or share, of the profit.

People had bought stock in companies they believed made a good product. They just wanted to share in the profits. Then they began to **gamble** on the price of stocks. People began to buy stocks just so they could sell them when their price went up. Not only wealthy people were "playing" the stock market this way, but also ordinary men and women, who invested their life savings in stocks. More and more people played the stock market, and they paid much more for stocks than they were actually worth. By the end of the 1920s, stocks were dangerously overvalued. The whole stock market was like a big bubble that grew and grew on nothing but air. The bubble burst in October 1929, when the price of stocks fell drastically. In 1931, a share in U.S. Steel that cost $262 in 1922 was later worth only $22.

People who had invested in the stock market began to panic. They tried to sell their stocks before the prices dropped even more. Unfortunately, with everyone trying to sell, almost no one was buying. The Black Tuesday stock market "crash" led to the Great Depression of the 1930s.

Millions of people lost the houses and cars for which they could no longer afford to pay. Americans were afraid they would lose all their money, so they withdrew all of it from the banks. That meant the banks couldn't loan money to people or companies to buy anything. Since no one could buy anything, factories had to **lay off** their workers. The laid-off workers could not afford to buy things made by other workers, so more factories shut down.

By the end of 1932, the disaster had descended through the entire American economy, and about one in four Americans had no job. Millions of Americans could not pay for the bare necessities. Thousands of people stood in the cold, in "bread lines" that stretched for blocks, just to be served a bowl of soup, or a piece of bread. Men who once might have owned their own businesses or worked in an office stood behind crates of apples, selling the fruit to earn a few cents.

On the outskirts of large cities, hundreds of homeless people crowded into tents and **shanties** made of scraps of wood and metal. They gathered in **makeshift** villages called "Hoovervilles"—after President Herbert Hoover. The hungriest people picked through the dumps for something to eat. Many Americans blamed Republican President Herbert Hoover for the Depression. A "Hoover flag" was an empty pocket turned inside out. "Hoover blankets" were the newspapers under which homeless people slept.

This was not completely fair. President Hoover became famous for leading the effort to send food to hungry Europeans after World War I. After the crash, he helped business owners get loans, and urged them not to lay off workers. Hoover and most Republicans however, believed in America's traditional free enterprise system. He believed that individuals, not the government, should make most of the economic decisions, and individuals should be responsible for themselves.

He authorized the building of the Hoover Dam, which provided electricity and flood control, and a regular water supply, to the people in the Colorado River basin. That, in turn, helped expand the California agricultural industry. Hoover refused to consider the idea that government should aid the unemployed directly with jobs.

Voters did not re-elect him in 1932. They chose Democrat Franklin Delano Roosevelt, FDR, in his place. Roosevelt, Teddy Roosevelt's fifth cousin, had a bold plan, called the "New Deal," to get people through the Depression.

Roosevelt, in an exciting, emotional inaugural speech, urged Americans to maintain hope and courage. He said his greatest task was to put people to work. His New Deal had 3 Rs: Relief, Recovery and Reform. The New Deal was a bold plan, but it did not immediately end the Depression. Hard times continued through the decade.

He first reformed the banking system by **insuring** bank deposits. If the bank lost a depositor's money, the federal government replaced it. This was the beginning of the Federal Deposit Insurance Corporation (FDIC) and

Passing Out Bread During the Depression

the Securities and Exchange Commission (SEC), which oversees the stock market now.

Then, a **devastating drought** in 1934 and 1935 hit the farms on the Great Plains, the "nation's breadbasket" that covers parts of Texas, Oklahoma, Kansas, Nebraska, Colorado and the Dakotas. The soil got so dry that it blew away on the wind, sometimes making a sunny day as dark as the middle of the night. There was so much dust in the air that people had to wear a cloth over their mouths to keep from **choking**. As dust storm followed dust storm, people all over the country began to call the **formerly** rich farmland, the Dust Bowl.

The farmers of the Great Plains had already suffered the effects of the Depression, along with everyone else, but now their farms were blowing away. Thousands of farm families fled westward, hoping to find jobs on the

A Typical Vehicle Driven by an 'Okie" on the Way to California

rich farms of California. They became migrant (traveling) workers, working at temporary, low-paid jobs. They would pick fruit at harvest time and then be jobless the rest of the year. They lived in their cars or in miserable camps along the roadside.

New **Social Security** protections did not cover farm workers, so the migrant farm workers got little or no help from the government, despite the New Deal. Many people consider the "Okies" (the workers from Oklahoma) examples of how terrible things had become in America. Once proud and self-sufficient farmers, they were now living like **serfs**. Author John Steinbeck wrote one of the most famous American novels, *The Grapes of Wrath*, about the suffering and endurance of migrant workers (see Appendix F).

One New Deal relief program was the Civilian Conservation Corps (CCC). It gave jobs to men 18-25 years old, to work on projects that improved and protected the environment. Living in camps on public lands, or in the national parks, the CCC workers built trails and bridges, stopped soil erosion, fought forest fires and planted millions of acres of trees. The work was hard, but it was useful and many young men learned many job skills.

Many of these projects were in the Great Plains. The government hoped the trees would hold the soil down and prevent another Dust Bowl disaster. The CCC gave millions of frustrated, jobless young men a new sense of pride and satisfaction along with their jobs.

The Works Progress Administration (WPA), an even bigger jobs program, employed construction workers and engineers on new building projects all over the country. Government money was used to build or improve roads, bridges, power plants, school buildings, hospitals and airports. The WPA also employed artists. Musicians and actors performed in large and small communities, some of which had never seen a professional play or concert. Writers wrote guidebooks about different parts of the country. Painters splashed colorful murals on the walls of public buildings. Never before had the U.S. government done so much for and with the arts.

Roosevelt's New Deal programs went beyond job creation. One program, the Tennessee Valley Authority (TVA), was designed to improve the lives of millions of people in the poverty-stricken Tennessee Valley in parts of seven southern states. The TVA taught farmers better ways to grow crops. It constructed great dams along the rivers to protect against the flooding that often destroyed the farmers' crops. The TVA **harnessed** the power of the rivers with power plants that delivered electricity to the homes in the area. Before the TVA, only two of every 100 local homes had electric power.

One of the most remarkable engineering achievements of the 20th century, the Golden Gate suspension bridge, stretches 4,200 feet across the entrance to the San Francisco Bay at the Pacific Ocean. It was built during the Depression, but without New Deal money. Like the Statue of Liberty, the Golden Gate Bridge has become a symbol of American dreams.

Some people mocked the new agencies that were known by their initials, like the CCC, WPA, TVA and many more. They joked that Roosevelt had cooked up a big pot of "alphabet soup." Others, especially the poor, understood that America takes care of her own.

Once the economy began to recover, Roosevelt turned his attention to making sure that workers received a fair wage, and that child labor was eliminated. He created **subsidies** to give farmers fair prices for their food. Congress passed the Wagner Act in 1935 to protect workers' rights to join labor unions, and the right of unions to negotiate with employers. Later, the Fair Labor Standards Act established the maximum working hours per week, **minimum** wage rates and **banned** child labor.

The Golden Gate Bridge over San Francisco Bay

Social Security was perhaps the most important New Deal program. Before Social Security, Americans worried that they would not be able to support themselves if they got injured or when they got old. A worker who lost his job could turn to charity or "relief," but many Americans were ashamed to ask for help. They believed that people should take care of themselves.

Congress approved the Social Security Act in 1935. Most workers now had to pay a small part of their income into a special government fund. Then, if the worker got injured at work, the government would pay him money out of the fund so he could support himself until he recovered from the injury. If the worker was unable to return to work because of the injury or because he **retired**, the government used the fund to send him small, but regular, payments for the rest of his life. Americans now believed that even if they were injured and couldn't work or grew too old to work, they would survive. They were not ashamed to take Social Security, because they had paid for this benefit.

Roosevelt also agreed to allow **deficit spending** for the U.S.—to allow the country to spend more money that it received in taxes—but he didn't like it. Roosevelt thought deficit spending should only be used during great economic crises. He agreed because he thought the position would help kick-start the economy by giving money directly to the people so they could buy goods and services again.

Many people believe the New Deal marked a turning point in the Depression and American history. It expanded the power of government, and gave it a more active role in the shaping the economy. The government was more involved in taking care of its citizens.

Roosevelt is the only president to be elected four times, in 1932, 1936, 1940 and 1944.

Roosevelt had great energy and imagination. He also communicated effectively and directly with Americans in weekly "fireside chats" on the radio. He **informally** explained public issues in clear, simple language, and then explained how his New Deal would fix the problem. Roosevelt was not popular with everyone. Some Americans thought he was grabbing too much power. Wealthy Americans, especially hated Roosevelt, because they thought his economic ideas were destroying free enterprise.

The president came from a very wealthy background. He never suffered poverty, but he knew about personal hardship. He was stricken with polio at age 39, which **paralyzed** his legs. Vaccines have mostly eliminated polio now, but it caused terrible suffering through the 1950s. Doctors thought he would have to give up his political career, but FDR refused. He exercised his upper body despite great pain. He gradually regained control and power in his arms. His legs never really improved. He spent the rest of his life in a wheelchair, or using **braces** and **crutches** to stand. He hid his disabilities from the public because he was afraid people would not understand that he could still do the job.

Roosevelt's wife, Eleanor, was a **remarkable** First Lady. Eleanor was especially concerned about the nation's poor people, women and African-Americans. She traveled all over the country, becoming her husband's "eyes and ears" among Americans because he could not travel easily. She often invited African-American leaders to dinner at the White House. This action shocked many people, especially in the South, where whites and blacks were still strictly **segregated**.

At a meeting in Birmingham, Alabama, where the audience was divided into white and black sections, the First Lady sat in the black section with a friend. When officials asked her to move to the white section, she moved her chair to the aisle between the two sections. Eleanor also urged her husband to appoint more women to important government positions.

During the New Deal years, the federal government also passed the Indian Reorganization Act, called the "Indian New Deal." In 1934, the Indian

Listening to One of FDR's Fireside Chats

Reorganization Act stopped Indian land allotments and provided money to buy land for the Native American tribes. The Commissioner of Indian Affairs, John Collier, worked tirelessly to get this act passed. Collier's plan also gave tribes some power to govern themselves.

The War Years

During most of the 1930s, Americans were too worried about problems at home to pay attention to the rest of the world, even when the Great Depression spread to Europe. In Germany, where more than one-third of the German workers lost their jobs, the suffering was especially serious. Many Germans were starving. Their money was worthless. It took a wheelbarrow full of German money to buy a loaf of bread. Like Americans, Germans wanted a strong leader.

In 1933, the same year Roosevelt first took office, Adolf Hitler became the German chancellor—like a president—but he was a very different kind of leader. Hitler quickly declared himself the absolute **dictator** of Germany. There was only one political party, his National Socialist German Workers' (or Nazi) Party. Hitler declared the beginning of a great new era in German history, the Third Reich, or empire. Hitler promised that the Third Reich would make Germany the most powerful nation in the world. Hitler put unemployed citizens to work just like Roosevelt. However, unlike Roosevelt, he put them to work making military weapons and vehicles. He planned to make the German army powerful enough to conquer all of Europe.

Hitler and the Nazis gained power partly by making the Germans feel proud, and partly by stirring up hatred. They encouraged hatred of the nations—Britain, France and the United States—that had defeated Germany in World War I. Above all, Hitler stirred up hate against a minority group in Germany: Jews. Hitler blamed all of Germany's problems on the Jews. He considered them to be an **inferior** race that was trying to take over Germany. In 1935, the German government systematically **persecuted** Jews, eliminating the Jews' civil rights, and forbidding Jews to marry anyone who was not Jewish.

In 1938, Hitler **launched** his attempt to conquer the world. The German army first conquered Austria (where Hitler was born) in 1938, followed by the country that, until recently, was called Czechoslovakia.

Britain and France watched nervously. They were close enough to be **invaded**, too. When Germany invaded Poland in September 1939, Britain

German Advances
World War II
1938–1941

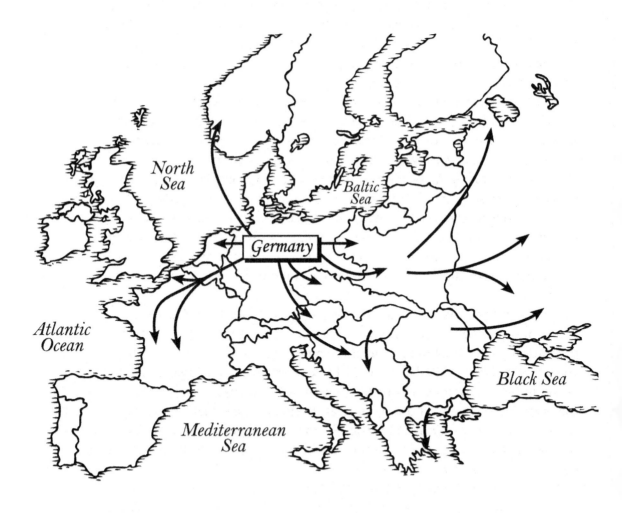

and France declared war on Germany. The Second World War (World War II) had begun, and Germany appeared to be unstoppable.

Hitler's powerful army moved across the continent in fast attacks they called **blitzkrieg**, or "lightning war." In April 1940, the Germans conquered Denmark and Norway. The next month they captured Belgium and Holland, and then invaded France. Within weeks the German army did what it had failed to do during all the years of World War I. It conquered France.

Now Hitler dominated almost all of Europe. Britain stood alone in its resistance. Britain was an island, making an army invasion difficult. For months, in what came to be known as the Battle of Britain, the Germans **rained** bombs on England, killing thousands and destroying ancient cities. The British in the cities sent their children to safety in the countryside, but refused to give in.

Winston Churchill, the British prime minister, famously declared in 1940 that " ... we shall never surrender." Churchill also predicted that sooner or later, as in World War I, America would once again rescue Europe.

Most Americans sympathized with Britain's lonely fight, but after the horrors of World War I, many remained isolationists. Roosevelt, however, considered Germany's actions a threat to democracy. He convinced Congress that America should help Britain by sending weapons and supplies. He said an intelligent person would lend a garden hose to a neighbor whose house is on fire—before the fire spread to his own house.

He also said America had to build up its own defenses. The American military became small and weak after World War I, so FDR began to rebuild it. All over the country factories began building ships, planes and tanks. Almost a million men were drafted into the military. With all the new jobs, the economy finally began to recover from the Depression.

For the sake of democracy, Americans were willing to **stockpile** an "arsenal," or collection, of weapons. However, they were not willing to fight. Finally, when there was a military attack on American soil and American naval ships, the Americans decided to enter the war.

A group of military men came to power in Japan in the 1920s a little before the Nazis started growing and taking control of Germany. Just as the Nazis dreamed of ruling Europe, this new military government dreamed of ruling Asia. In 1937, the Japanese launched an invasion of much-larger China. The Chinese, under Gen. Chiang Kai-shek, fought fiercely. However, after three years of bloody fighting, the Japanese finally controlled much of eastern China. Japan allied itself with Germany the same year.

The Three Axis Powers

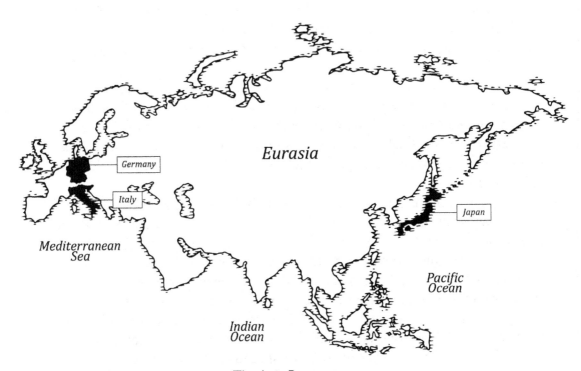

The Axis Powers

During this time, Italy was ruled by a dictator named Benito Mussolini, known as "Il Duce," or "the leader." Mussolini led the Fascist Party, a Nazi-like group that stirred up fierce national pride in Italians, along with a hatred of foreigners. These three countries—Germany, Japan and Italy—joined together. They were called the Axis Powers.

Roosevelt was concerned about the Japanese advance. He called Japan an "aggressor nation" that was as dangerous as Germany. In summer 1941, Japan occupied Indochina (now North and South Vietnam, Laos and Cambodia). Roosevelt banned the **export** of oil, iron and rubber to Japan, and warned that trade would not resume until the Japanese withdrew from China and Indochina. Japan responded with a devastating surprise attack on Pearl Harbor, a U.S. Navy base on the island of Oahu in Hawaii, the headquarters of the Navy's Pacific Ocean fleet.

Few men were on duty at Pearl Harbor on the sunny, peaceful Sunday morning of December 7, 1941. Then, five minutes before 8 a.m., planes filled the sky. At first, the men on the ground thought that the U.S. Air Force was practicing, but then they spotted a red circle painted on the planes. It was the rising sun of Japan's flag.

Men rushed to their duty stations while the Japanese pilots dove at them. The important targets for the Japanese were the American warships lined up in the harbor. Bombs and torpedoes **slammed** into the ships and the base, while crews scrambled to get to their anti-aircraft guns. One Japanese pilot landed a direct hit on the battleship USS Arizona. More than 1,100 of the 1,777 American sailors onboard were killed, or thrown into the water to drown. The attack lasted two hours. By the time the Japanese pilots flew away, they had sunk or badly damaged 19 ships and killed more than 2,000 Americans.

Americans were shocked and angry about the surprise attack on Pearl Harbor. The day after the attack, President Roosevelt declared December 7, 1941 "a date which will live in **infamy**," and asked Congress to declare war on Japan. Congress agreed immediately.

Just days later, Japan's allies, Germany and Italy, also declared war on the United States. American isolationism disappeared overnight. Millions of young men and some women—rushed to join the military. America joined the allied British, French, Chinese and Soviets (Russians) in World

The Bombing of Pearl Harbor

War II against the Axis Powers. Though France had been conquered, there was a group of Frenchmen of the Free French who refused to accept German rule. They fought on the side of the Allies.

General Charles de Gaulle, a World War I hero, led the Free French. De Gaulle escaped to England and organized a fighting force of Frenchmen living overseas. He also directed civilian French men and women in the French Resistance in an underground war against the Germans.

Americans believed that fighting the Axis powers would **preserve** democracy, even though one of America's allies was not democratic. Brutal dictator, Joseph Stalin, ruled the Soviet Union. He killed millions of Russians. The Allies accepted Stalin, despite his human rights crimes, because they considered the Axis powers a more direct threat. Stalin's crimes could wait until after the war. The politics of war sometimes leads to unnatural alliances.

In August 1939, Hitler and Stalin signed the Nazi-Soviet Non-Aggression Pact—"we won't attack you, if you don't attack us." The agreement would have allowed Germany and the Soviet Union to take over and divide a country they both wanted: Poland. In early September 1939, Germany invaded Poland from the west, while the Soviet Union invaded from the east. Poland quickly surrendered. The Soviets moved into the neighboring countries in the north—Latvia, Lithuania and Estonia—with **strategic** access to the Baltic Sea.

Even though Hitler and Stalin agreed to divide Poland, this action did not make them friends. In 1941, German troops violated the pact, invaded the Soviet Union, and made the Soviets switch sides to join the Allies. The Axis powers seemed to be winning when America entered the war. Germany had fought its way to within 25 miles of the Soviet capital city, Moscow. In northern Africa, German forces were fighting the British for possession of Egypt (which was then a British colony) and access to oil fields.

The Japanese were equally successful on the other side of the world. Within months of the attack on Pearl Harbor, they conquered the rest of Southeast Asia. After moving down the Malay Peninsula, they conquered the Dutch East Indies (called Indonesia today). They invaded Burma (called Myanmar today) in the West and the Philippine Islands in the East. The former American territory still had large numbers of American troops **stationed** there. American and Filipino forces resisted for six months, but at last, they were forced to surrender.

Wherever Germans ruled, the conquered lived in terror, but no group suffered as much from German cruelty as the Jews. The Nazis built prison and concentration camps in Germany and Poland in the early 1940s. The concentration camps, also called death camps, were killing factories. Jewish men, women and children—and some Catholics, homosexuals and gypsies—were herded like cattle into large rooms called gas chambers. Poison gas was pumped into the rooms and killed everyone in minutes.

The mass murder of the Jews is known as the Holocaust, which means total destruction. The Holocaust was one of the worst attempts at **genocide** in the history of the world. Six million Jews were murdered, two-thirds of the Jewish population in Europe.

During the war, few Americans knew about the death camps. They learned about them when American troops entered the camps at the end of the war. Even the toughest soldiers were shocked by what they found. In one camp they found a bin full of thousands of pairs of tiny shoes, taken from Jewish babies before they were killed. Some Jews were found alive—so starved that they looked like walking skeletons.

In 1942, President Roosevelt and British Prime Minister Churchill put their armies under a single command. Invasion on the ground would have to wait. They would bomb Germany as Germany had bombed Britain, to weaken the will to fight in the German people. The bombing caused major damage in Germany, including many civilian deaths.

That summer, Germany launched a massive **assault** against Stalingrad in the southern Soviet Union. Hitler thought he could defeat the Soviet Union by gaining control of the great natural resources of southern Russia, including wheat and oil. First, German planes bombed much of the city to **rubble**. When the German army moved in on the ground, Russians

German Concentration Camp

met them with rifles and bayonets. The Germans paid for every inch of ground that they won. After that, two large Russian forces surrounded the Germans, and pounded the trapped enemy with artillery. Then winter came.

Russian winters are infamous for their terrible cold and great snowstorms. The German forces surrendered in February 1943, finally defeated by the Russian winter. The Battle of Stalingrad was the first great German defeat, and it changed the course of the war. Another Allied victory, more than a thousand miles from the snows of Stalingrad, in the **blazing desert** of North Africa, helped. British troops stopped the Germans in the battle at El Alamein in Egypt. Now everyone started to believe that the Germans could be beaten.

The world's largest ocean, the Pacific, separates Japan and the United States. When America finally entered World War II, Japan dominated the western half of the ocean. Then in June 1942, the Japanese attacked Midway, a group of islands occupied by the United States. The Japanese and American navies **clashed** off Midway in a new kind of naval battle, one fought by planes rather than ships. Planes took off from the decks of ships called aircraft carriers and attacked enemy ships. The Japanese lost their four best aircraft carriers in the battle and were forced to retreat. The Battle of Midway stopped the Japanese advance across the Pacific.

Now the Americans began the long process of "island hopping," fighting their way across one island after another. Repeatedly, the Japanese fought to the death, refusing to surrender. Americans spent three years taking islands one by one, moving slowly toward Japan.

Back in the United States, everyone joined the war effort. Civilians bought bonds to help pay for the war by loaning the country money. They accepted shortages of things like meat and gasoline, which had to be sent to the soldiers overseas. People worked night and day in factories, building planes, ships, vehicles and weapons for British, Russian and American armies.

With so many young men away at war, many women went to work in the factories. About 6 million women joined the labor force, many of them in jobs using and making heavy machinery, something women had never done before. A symbol of these women was a fictional character named "Rosie the **Riveter**," who **flexed** the muscles in her arms to show her strength.

The war stirred up powerful anger that led to American injustices committed against Japanese Americans. Many Japanese Americans lived on America's West Coast. Since Pearl Harbor, some Americans had become enraged at the Japanese, or afraid of Japanese Americans, who they thought could be spies loyal to Japan.

Rosie the Riveter Model for a War Poster

President Roosevelt signed an "extraordinary order" in 1942 that **interned** Japanese American families who had done nothing wrong. More than 110,000 Japanese American men, woman and children lost their homes and property and were locked into guarded, fenced camps. Another 2,000 Germans and Italians in America were also interned in camps. Their families were given the choice to join them, but Japanese Americans—many of them born here—had no choice. Even though many Japanese Americans fought for the United States in Europe, the government did not release Japanese Americans until late 1944.

Today, most Americans consider the interments an injustice. Only people of Asian descent were locked up, suspected of being disloyal simply because they looked Japanese. The United States fought for human rights abroad while it violated the rights of thousands of innocent people at home.

American General Dwight D. Eisenhower commanded the Allied troops. At dawn on June 6, 1944, later called "D-Day," 156,000 Allied troops, 73,000 of them American, began **swarming** the beaches of Normandy, France. Within five days, over 300,000 troops had landed on five Normandy beaches in occupied northern France. Thousands of Allied and Axis troops were killed. In some places, the Allies quickly overran the outnumbered Germans, but at Omaha Beach, American troops met with fierce resistance. The beach was covered with German mines, barbed wire and "pillboxes," small defensive earthworks or embankments with machine-gunners inside.

The Battle of Omaha Beach on D-Day During World War II

German artillery fired down on the landing craft from cliffs above the beach. Slowly and bloodily, Americans fought ashore. A small, daring group of U.S. Rangers climbed the cliffs with ropes, and destroyed the German guns to slow the **slaughter**.

After a long day of fighting, the Allies had taken the beaches of Normandy and moved about a mile inland. Over the next few months, a vast wave of troops would push the Germans out of France. By October, most of the country was **liberated**. At the same time, the Soviets quickly moved across Eastern Europe. All that remained of the Nazi empire by early 1945 was Germany itself.

In February 1945, the three main Allied leaders, Churchill, Roosevelt and Stalin, met at Yalta in the Soviet Union to discuss what would happen after the war. They agreed that Germany would be occupied by troops from all the Allied nations. It would be divided into four parts, each run by one of the occupiers: Britain, the United States, France and the Soviet Union.

Churchill and Roosevelt were also concerned about the future of the Soviet-occupied Eastern European nations. Churchill was especially worried that Nazi domination of Eastern Europe would be replaced by Soviet domination. Pressured by the other Allied leaders, Stalin finally agreed to allow free elections in Eastern Europe after the war.

In April 1945, FDR fell unconscious while he posed for a painting. He died several days later, on April 12. Americans mourned the man who had led them through the long years of the Depression and war, only to die with victory in sight.

Vice President Harry S. Truman succeeded Roosevelt. Although the new president, a former clothing salesman, felt the heavy weight of his unexpected responsibilities, he proved to be a tough, effective leader.

The war in Europe was ending. Russian armies invaded Germany from the east while British and American armies invaded from the west. A few days after the Allied armies met at the Elbe River, Hitler was dead. The German dictator, who had launched the world into war, shot himself on April 30 to avoid capture. On May 7, 1945, Germany surrendered.

That left only Japan.

In April 1945, Americans launched on attack on Okinawa (a large, heavily defended island 400 miles south of Japan). It took American troops 82 days to fight the 70-mile length of the island. Shortly after they captured Okinawa, American troops learned that Germany had surrendered, but the Japanese refused to quit. Japan retreated from its conquered territories, but still had two million soldiers in Japan. President Truman believed that Japan could be invaded only at a huge cost in American lives. To force a Japanese surrender, Truman ordered the military to drop two atomic bombs on Japan.

In the 1930s, scientists discovered that splitting the nucleus of certain heavy atoms, like uranium-235 and plutonium-239, releases an **inconceivable** amount of energy. Scientists began working on a way to use this energy in a "super bomb" more powerful than any weapon that had ever existed.

As the war continued, the U.S. invested millions of dollars in the attempt. The Manhattan Project was created in 1942 to coordinate all the individual scientists working on the atomic bomb. The first atomic bomb was **detonated** in the New Mexico desert in July 1945. It exploded with the force of 13,000 tons of ordinary explosives. The desert flooded with a light brighter than the sun, the ground rocked as if struck by an earthquake, and then a hurricane-force wind swept across the desert. The explosion released huge amounts of deadly radiation. The scientists saw a giant, mushroom-shaped cloud rise high into the air.

The first bomb was dropped on the city of Hiroshima, on August 6, 1945. More than 80,000 people died in the first flash of the gigantic fireball. Thousands died later from burns or from radiation contamination, an effect that was mostly unknown at the time. Almost the entire city burned to the ground. Japan still rejected American demands for surrender. The U.S. dropped a second atomic bomb on the city of Nagasaki three days later. Finally, the Japanese government, fearing the destruction of the entire country, surrendered.

World War II was finally over. In six years of conflict, an estimated 40 million people lost their lives all over the world. A terrifying new weapon had ended the most terrible war in history.

The Bombing of Hiroshima

Becoming a
World Example
1946-1992

Tribute to Self-Government

After World War II, the United States and the Soviet Union were the most powerful nations in the world. The "superpowers" had fought as allies, but opposed each other after the war. The United States is a democratic country whose citizens freely elect its government, and where individual rights are guaranteed by a constitution. The Soviet Union was a **totalitarian** state. The government controlled every part of its citizens' economic, political and social lives. Soviet citizens were denied freedom of speech, freedom of the press and freedom of religion.

The American and Soviet economic systems were also very different. America is a capitalist country, in which private citizens control their own economic actions. The Soviet Union, however, was communist—the government controlled all property and economic activity.

In 1945, the United Nations (U.N.) replaced the League of Nations. This time, the United States joined the international peacekeeping organization. The first permanent members of the U.N. Security Council were France, the Republic of China, the Soviet Union, the United Kingdom and the United States.

The Soviet Union established communist governments across Eastern Europe after World War II. In 1946, Churchill said that an "iron curtain" now separated Eastern communist governments from Western democratic governments. He meant that Europe was now separated into two parts and the imaginary barrier was very obvious. He asked the democracies to resist Soviet aggression and communism.

President Truman promised in 1947 that the United States would help any country to resist, if threatened by communism. The *Truman Doctrine* was tested for the first time in Greece, where communists tried to overthrow the government. The U.S. sent American officers to help the Greek army, and gave money to Greece for military equipment. The army defeated the communists in late 1949.

Many European cities, factories and roads were in ruins after World War II. So, the United States created the Marshall Plan, named after U.S.

The United Nations Building

Secretary of State George C. Marshall in 1948. The U.S. spent billions of dollars to rebuild the Western European economy, because that would also help the world economy. The U.S. also had another motivation. This plan helped assure that Britain, France, West Germany and Italy would side with America in the event of another war.

In 1949, 12 nations: Belgium, Denmark, France, Great Britain, Iceland, Italy, Luxembourg, the Netherlands, Norway, Portugal, the United States and Canada formed a defensive alliance. Members promised each other military support if any other member was attacked. This alliance was called the North Atlantic Treaty Organization (NATO), and it was the first time the United States formed an alliance during peacetime.

The United States and the Soviet Union did engage in another war, but it was a different type of war. It wasn't a "hot" war with bombs and bullets. It was a long, tense "cold" war that often came dangerously close to real war.

From 1946 to 1991, the Soviet Union encouraged communism in China and other nations. The United States helped countries resist communism. The United States supported democratic governments, but also sometimes supported dictators—if they were anti-communist.

The United States and Soviet Union both greatly increased their military forces during the Cold War. Most Americans accepted the increase to protect the country and its allies. Some people, however, were afraid that the military and the businesses that built weapons and supplies were gaining too much political power.

This group included General Dwight D. Eisenhower, who had led the Allied World War II troops in Europe. Americans considered him a hero, so they elected him president in 1952 and 1956. When he left office in 1961, he warned Americans that the combined power of the military and the weapons industry could threaten democracy.

The greatest threat of the Cold War, however, was nuclear war. America became the first nuclear power in 1945, but four years later Americans were shocked when the Soviets tested their first atomic bomb. Americans feared the Soviets might try to use nuclear bombs on the U.S.

President Truman announced that America would build a more powerful kind of nuclear weapon, the hydrogen bomb, or "H-bomb." The H-bomb would work by fusion, which would slam atoms together, rather than by fission, which split atoms apart. An H-bomb would release far more energy than an atomic bomb.

An H-bomb was tested on a deserted Pacific island in 1954. It was 1,000 times more powerful than the atom bomb the U.S. dropped on Hiroshima and Nagasaki. It released enough radiation to kill every living thing in an area the size of New Jersey.

The Soviets, however, had also discovered how to make an H-bomb. Now Americans and Soviets tried to stay ahead of each other by building more and more powerful nuclear weapons in a nuclear arms race.

The arms race frightened many Americans. Some families thought they could survive if they dug bomb shelters deep underground. Children in American schools learned to "**duck and cover**" in hallways and under their desks. They were told they were doing "tornado drills," but the drills were really supposed to save them in an atomic bomb attack.

Americans considered 1949 one of the most dangerous years of the Cold War. Soviets developed the atomic bomb, and a group of communists took over the government of China, the most **populous** country in the world.

All this created fear and suspicion in Americans. Suspected communists were denied government jobs, even with little or no evidence that they really were communists.

Republican Sen. Joseph McCarthy used this fear and suspicion to gain power. In February 1950, McCarthy said that 205 people in the Secretary of State's offices were communists. McCarthy had no such list of people. The false accusations, however, made him famous. So, in 1951 he **accused**

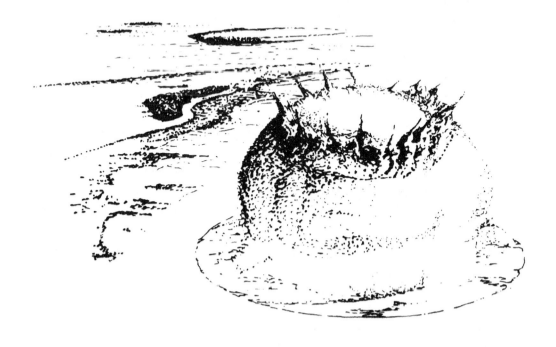

H-Bomb Exploding on a Coral Atoll

the Secretary of Defense of leading a communist plot to take over the government. This charge was also false, but the Defense Secretary was forced to quit his job. McCarthy's **smear** tactic became known as "McCarthyism."

In the mid-1950s, America turned against McCarthy, after he claimed that the U.S. Army was protecting communists. McCarthy's televised speeches helped most Americans understand that McCarthy was nothing but a **bully** and a liar. The Senate condemned McCarthy, and his own Republican Party turned against him.

In the early 1950s, the Cold War went hot for several years when American troops fought communists in Korea. Korea lies on a peninsula between China and Japan. After World War II, the Americans occupied the southern half of the country while the Soviets occupied the north.

In June 1950, the communist North Korean army invaded South Korea. North Korea quickly captured the South Korean capital of Seoul. The United States and the U.N. sent American troops to defend South Korea. Three months after the invasion, a large U.N. force, more than 90 percent American, landed near Seoul and recaptured the city. By the end of October, U.N. troops had pushed all the way through North Korea to the border with China.

It appeared Korea might now be reunited as a democracy, but that changed when communist China joined the war. At the end of November 1950, thousands of Chinese troops poured into North Korea. The outnumbered Americans were driven back and, within a month, U.N. forces were driven back into South Korea. Fighting continued at the original border.

American General Douglas MacArthur wanted to attack China, but President Truman refused to let him. Truman didn't want to risk war with China's ally, the Soviet Union, because that could start World War III. This war would be worse than the first two wars, because both sides now had nuclear weapons. The two sides fought to a **stalemate** in June 1951, but fighting continued until 1953.

Korea remains divided today. Some Americans are frustrated that the war ended without a clear victory, but others considered the Korean War a success. The United States stood up to communist aggression and avoided war with the Soviet Union.

Despite the overseas battles, the 1950s were optimistic and prosperous for most Americans. The Second World War hurt the economies of Europe and Asia, but lifted the United States out of the Depression and put most people back to work. Unlike Europe and Asia, the U.S. did not have to

Korea

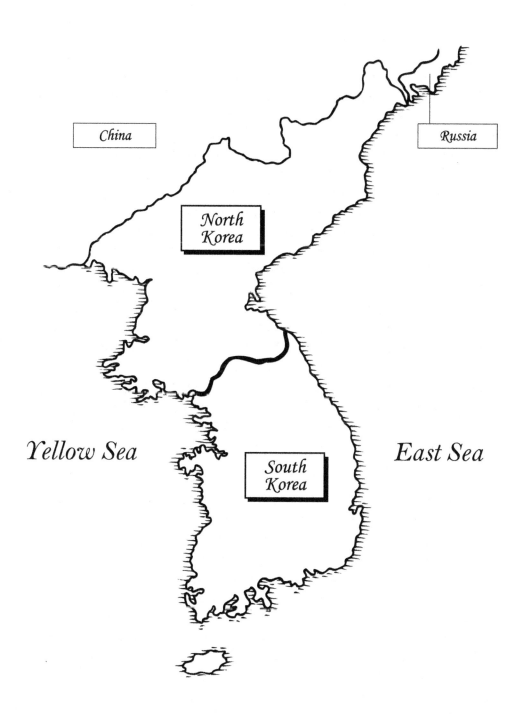

China

Russia

North
Korea

Yellow Sea

East Sea

South
Korea

rebuild cities, roads and factories. The Marshall Plan also created a strong overseas market for U.S. products.

During World War II, most American factory goods were sent overseas for the soldiers. People who had saved their money during the war wanted to start buying again. Millions of fighting men were coming home, too. They were eager to buy new cars, get married and buy new houses and electrical appliances. Industry boomed with this demand for new goods.

In 1944 Congress created the "GI Bill of Rights." Europeans had called soldiers "GIs," **slang** for "government-issue" servicemen. The GI Bill paid the veterans' college **tuition** and the **fees** charged by universities. Millions of veterans went to college who would not have been able to go without the bill. The GI Bill also gave veterans government loans to buy their own homes. Millions of new homes were built all over the country. By the end of the 1950s, 60 percent of Americans owned their own homes. Most of the new houses were built just outside existing cities, creating suburbs. Soon, these large, middle-class communities surrounded most major cities.

The growth of the suburbs changed American lifestyles. It made the automobile more important than ever. The new communities usually had no mass transportation, like buses or trains, so by the end of the 1950s, 75 percent of American families owned a car. As a result, Congress voted in 1956 to build a vast system of interstate highways, roads at least four lanes wide, to crisscross the country. The interstate highway program was the largest building program ever undertaken by any government. Americans embraced driving on the big, fast, new roads in big, new cars.

Americans also spent their money on **gadgets** intended to make life easier—everything from washing machines to electric knives. Electricity use tripled during the 1950s.

The gadget that really changed American life was the television. Scientists had been experimenting with TV since the 1920s, but it wasn't until the late 1940s that the technology finally took off. There wasn't much to watch in the beginning. The early television programs were created in individual cities and they were broadcast just to that city.

National programming was created in the early 1950s, and suddenly everyone everywhere wanted a TV. Two-thirds of American homes had a black-and-white set by the mid-1950s. The most popular shows were silly comedies, children's shows or the adventures of detectives and cowboys. Some people began to refer TV as the "boob tube," but not everything on television was **junk**. People could watch history take place. People could see for themselves that Joseph McCarthy was just a liar and a bully.

People also began to support the Civil Rights Movement after they saw shocking pictures of African-Americans being attacked by police on television. John F. Kennedy was elected president in 1960, after people watched his opponent, Richard M. Nixon, sweating nervously in televised debates. Nixon didn't look trustworthy, but Kennedy appeared calm and handsome.

The National System of Interstate Highways
circa 1950

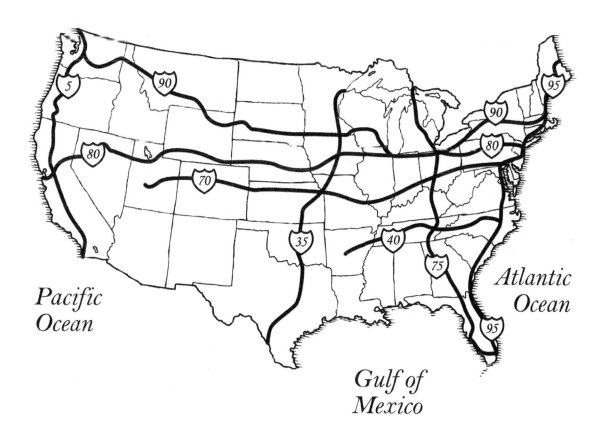

Pacific Ocean

Atlantic Ocean

Gulf of Mexico

Civil Rights in Post-World War II America

While the 1950s were good for most Americans, African-Americans did not enjoy the general prosperity or sense of victory and freedom that most whites experienced. From the beginning of American history, most blacks had lived in the southern states, where their ancestors had been taken as slaves. About 90 percent of all African-Americans still lived in the South in 1900. Many blacks looking for new opportunities moved north during and after World War I. That stream turned into a flood after World War II. By 1950, almost 30 percent of African-Americans had left the South. Many who went north discovered they still were not treated like equals.

More than 90 years after the Civil War, most blacks still did not have the basic right to vote in the South. Some African-Americans were told they had to pay a "poll tax" in order to vote. This was a fee that most blacks were too poor to pay. Sometimes they were forced to take difficult tests that white voters did not have to take. Some African-Americans were simply threatened with violence if they tried to vote.

Blacks in the South were also segregated—not allowed to mix with whites or even use white facilities like bathrooms and water fountains. They were refused housing in white neighborhoods and had to attend all-black schools.

Southern states passed hundreds of "Jim Crow" laws to **enforce** segregation. Some Jim Crow laws kept whites and blacks separate on buses and trains. Blacks had to sit in the rear of the bus, or stand if a white person needed a seat. They had to sit in the balcony at the movies. Some laws required hospitals to keep black patients in different sections from whites. Whites and blacks could not play on the same sports teams.

In the 1950s, African-Americans angry about Jim Crow laws energized the Civil Rights Movement to end segregation and other inequalities. The 1950s and 1960s saw the greatest successes of the Civil Rights Movement that had begun long ago.

African-American leaders like Frederick Douglass, during the Civil War, and later W.E.B. Du Bois, fought for equal rights for black Americans. From the 1920s to the 1950s, A. Philip Randolph led the largest black labor union, the union of railway porters. Porters helped train passengers during their journeys. Randolph didn't like the way black workers were treated during World War II. African-Americans worked in the factories that made weapons and vehicles for the Allies, but were limited to the lowest-paid jobs. Randolph asked President Roosevelt to make discrimination illegal. Roosevelt said he would study the problem, but didn't change anything.

Randolph said he would lead 100,000 African-Americans in a rally in Washington, D.C. to embarrass the U.S. into doing something. The United States was fighting German racism overseas. Randolph wanted to publicize the racism at home. As a result of Randolph's efforts, President Roosevelt banned discrimination against government and defense workers in June 1941.

African-Americans in the armed forces, however, remained segregated. Blacks were initially not even allowed to fight for their country—most were restricted to menial jobs like cooking, cleaning or serving officers. The few black soldiers who were allowed to fight served in all-black units. The black flying **squadron** called the

A Segregated Water Fountain in the South

Tuskegee Airmen, and the few allowed to fight in other roles, performed bravely and well. Randolph protested that most, however, were not allowed to fight for their country.

Randolph asked President Truman to integrate the armed forces in 1948. Like Roosevelt, Truman met Randolph, but changed nothing. So, Randolph urged young black men not to join the military. Truman finally gave in during July 1948. Two years later, black and white Americans fought side by side in the Korean War.

In the 1950s, the NAACP decided that public school segregation needed to end. Almost all schools in the South and many schools in the North were segregated. Southern states spent more money on white schools than they did on black schools, so Southern black children were at a disadvantage.

The NAACP decided to challenge that discrimination using the legal system. In 1954, African-American **attorney** Thurgood Marshall argued Brown v. Board of Education of Topeka before the U.S. Supreme Court. (The "v" stands for versus, meaning against.) Third-grader Linda Brown was not allowed to attend the local white elementary school in Topeka, Kansas. She was forced to attend a black school farther from home. Marshall argued that this discrimination violated the U.S. Constitution. The Supreme Court agreed that segregated schools violated the rights of African-American students.

Jim Crow schools tried to continue segregation, by claiming that their black schools were "separate but equal" to the white schools—that they were good enough for the black children. The Supreme Court disagreed. It said that even if the same amount of money was spent on black and white schools, segregation would still be unfair, because it told black children they were not good enough to go to school with white children.

Some black students were threatened and attacked when they enrolled in all-white schools, but Brown v. Board of Education was the beginning of the end of segregated education. This was a great victory for the NAACP and Thurgood Marshall. In 1967, Marshall became the first African-American associate justice of the United States Supreme Court. Other civil rights cases continued to arise throughout the 1950s and 1960s.

In December 1955, an African-American woman named Rosa Parks got on a city bus on her way home from work in Montgomery, Alabama. White people sat in the front of the bus in Montgomery, and blacks had to sit in the back. Parks sat down in a row of seats just behind the "whites only" section, but the bus was crowded. When more white people got on the bus and one of them couldn't find a seat in the white section, the bus driver ordered the entire first row of black passengers to give up their seats to a white man. Three of the black passengers obeyed, but Rosa Parks remained in her seat. She was tired after working all day and didn't want to stand. Police arrested Parks because she had broken the Jim Crow law.

African-Americans all over Montgomery **boycotted** the bus system. They refused to ride the buses until black and white passengers were treated equally. Since most bus passengers were black, the boycott cost the bus company a lot of money. For more than a year, blacks walked to work or used taxis owned by blacks, rather than ride the bus. In December 1956, the U.S. Supreme Court ruled that segregated buses violated the Constitution.

People all over the country were **impressed** by the determination of the Montgomery African-Americans. The young black minister who led the boycott—Dr. Martin Luther King Jr.—especially impressed them. King, 26, became a minister while he was still a student at Morehouse College. Later he went to Boston University, where he earned a doctor of philosophy degree, a Ph.D. (The title of "Dr." is given to individuals who earn a Ph.D.)

King was the most important of all civil rights leaders. He was highly educated, and a **spellbinding** speaker. King was also courageous, willing to risk jail and possibly death for the sake of his cause. He gained followers largely because he insisted on changing society with passive resistance, rather than violence. King wanted people to quietly but firmly refuse to

A Typical City Bus in the South

obey unjust laws. He believed that, if enough people practiced passive resistance, they could change unjust laws.

Since he was a Christian, he followed Christ's teachings that said you should love everyone, even those who want to harm you. In addition to being influenced by the great nonviolent Indian leader, Mahatma Gandhi, King also relied on the ideas of 19th-century American writer and philosopher Henry David Thoreau (see Appendix F).

Thoreau went to jail in 1846 for refusing to pay his taxes. He said he would not pay taxes to a government that allowed slavery and started a war to steal land from Mexico. Thoreau's powerful essay *Civil Disobedience* persuaded many people to seek peaceful resolutions to injustice. "If a law requires you to be the agent of injustice to another," Thoreau wrote, "then I say, break the law."

One very effective form of passive resistance used in the 1960s was the "sit-in." Four black college students sat down for a meal at a lunch counter in Greensboro, North Carolina in early 1960. They knew no one would take their orders, because only white customers were served there, but they sat there until closing time. The next day a larger group of students arrived to sit in. The day after that, more students came, until the diner was too full for white customers. The sit-ins brought national attention to Jim Crow laws. King enthusiastically supported this tactic. In October 1960, King was arrested for participating in a sit-in at an Atlanta department store.

In 1963, King led a campaign to end segregation in Birmingham, Alabama, which King called the most segregated city in America. King led boycotts, sit-ins and marches. Pictures of white police beating blacks and aiming powerful fire hoses at small black children were printed in newspapers and broadcast on TV. Many Americans condemned the cruelty and began to sympathize with African-American demands for equal rights. The city eventually agreed to end most segregation. King and his followers won, but their victory **extended** far beyond Birmingham. Now many Americans of all ages were convinced that just, new laws should be passed.

Congress considered a **sweeping** new law: the Civil Rights Act. Black labor leader A. Phillip Randolph supported the law by planning the largest demonstration ever held in Washington, D.C.—the March on Washington—for August 28, 1963. More than 200,000 people marched—about 25 percent of them white. They sang the **spiritual** civil rights anthem, "We Shall Overcome," as they marched. Then, the demonstrators gathered at the Lincoln Memorial. After other leaders had spoken, King passionately addressed the crowd and the millions more who were watching on television.

I have a Dream
Martin Luther King

*"So I say to you, my friends, that even though we must face
the difficulties of today and tomorrow, I still have a dream.
It is a dream deeply rooted in the American dream that one day
this nation will rise up and live out the true meaning of its creed—
we hold these truths to be self-evident, that all men are created equal ...*

*I have a dream that my four little children will one day live in a
nation where they will not be judged by the color of their skin
but by the content of their character.*

I have a dream today!"

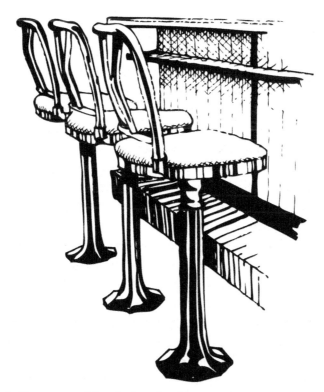

The Lunch Counter in North Carolina Where There was the First "Sit-In"

"… I have a dream that one day this nation will rise up, live out the true meaning of its creed: 'We hold these truths to be self-evident, that all men are created equal … ,'" he told Americans, who roared in agreement. The 1960s were interesting times for Americans. Not long before King's moving speech in Washington, the United States elected an inspiring young president with a beautiful, popular wife in 1960. John F. Kennedy, elected at the age of 43, is still the youngest president ever elected.

At his inauguration, he promised fresh new leadership. Kennedy was especially popular among young people. They responded to his call when he said, "Ask not what your country can do for you, ask what you can do for your country."

Thousands of idealistic young people joined Kennedy's new Peace Corps. Peace Corps members worked in poor countries, especially in Latin America and Africa. They helped build schools, roads and hospitals. Peace Corps volunteers made America many friends overseas—and some enemies, who were afraid the Peace Corps was run by spies.

The Cold War with the Soviet Union heated up during Kennedy's presidency. The United States and the Soviet Union quarreled over the German city of Berlin in 1961. Berlin, the largest German city, was located deep inside communist East Germany. Since World War II, British, French and American troops had occupied the western half of the city, which had become an island of democracy in a communist country. East Germans who did not want to be living under communism poured into West Berlin.

Soviet leader Nikita Khrushchev met with President Kennedy in 1961 and demanded that the United States and its allies leave the city. Kennedy refused. So, the Communists built a concrete wall between the two halves of the city. The wall was topped with barbed wire and guarded by soldiers who were ordered to shoot anyone who tried to escape East Berlin and East Germany. Almost 200 people were shot trying to escape over and under the wall over the next 30 years.

Berliners finally ended the symbol of tyranny in 1989, when the Communist East German government was overthrown. Demolition of the wall was completed in 1992.

The Soviets and the U.S. did not go to war over Berlin, but an even more dangerous conflict arose over Cuba, a Caribbean island. Revolutionaries overthrew a corrupt and **oppressive** government there in 1959. Fidel Castro promised to bring democracy to Cuba. Instead, he created a communist government allied with the Soviet Union. This action made Cuba the first communist country in the Western Hemisphere.

In October 1962, the U.S. government learned that the Soviets were building nuclear missile bases in Cuba, just 90 miles from the United States.

President Kennedy ordered the U.S. Navy to blockade the island nation, so the Soviets could not bring in more missiles.

A group of Soviet ships was already sailing to Cuba to confront the U.S. blockade. Everyone was waiting to see what would happen next. Suddenly, the Soviet ships turned around and headed home. Khrushchev offered to remove the missiles already in Cuba if Kennedy would end the blockade and agree not to invade the island. Soon the Soviets removed the missiles and left Cuba.

The world had come to the **brink** of nuclear war, but then backed away. In 1963, Americans began to work on agreements with the Soviet Union that controlled nuclear weapons, so that this would not happen again.

The Berlin Wall Separating East Berlin from West Berlin

The 1960s saw another competition heat up between the Soviets and the Americans—a "space race."

The Soviets got a head start. In 1957, they launched the first man-made satellite, Sputnik I, a small machine about twice the size of a basketball, into space on a rocket. They sent several more up over the next few years, sometimes with a dog or other small animal inside the satellite, and these satellites orbited the Earth. In 1961, the Soviets sent Yuri Gagarin—an astronaut—into space.

President Kennedy immediately dedicated himself to helping the U.S. win the space race. He asked Congress to designate billions of dollars to the new National Aeronautics and Space Administration (NASA). Kennedy challenged the country to land a man on the moon and return him safely to earth before 1970. After it sent monkeys and other small animals into space, NASA started training a group of military pilots as astronauts.

The astronauts quickly became heroes. Alan B. Shepard became the first American in space in May 1961. John Glenn became the first American to orbit the earth in February 1962. Glenn was given a big parade in New York City when he returned to Earth. He was also asked to speak to Congress—an honor usually only offered to leaders of foreign countries. Later in life, Glenn became a U.S. senator from Ohio.

On November 22, 1963, President Kennedy was assassinated in Dallas, Texas. He was shot as he rode in a convertible car with the top down. A government investigation concluded that the killer was a man named Lee Harvey Oswald. Oswald was shot and killed by another man two days after the assassination, so no one really knows why he killed Kennedy.

The president was given a funeral in Washington, D.C. Many Americans at home and around the world gathered around televisions to watch and mourn. Kennedy's coffin, guarded by soldiers, was drawn slowly through the streets on a caisson, a special horse-drawn cart. His three-year-old son saluted the casket as it passed.

After the assassination, Vice President Lyndon Baines Johnson became president. Johnson's background and personality were very different from Kennedy's. Johnson's family was middle-class Texans, while Kennedy came from a wealthy Massachusetts family. Kennedy went to Harvard, the most famous university in the country. Johnson went to a small Texas college. Kennedy dressed elegantly. Johnson wore cowboy hats and boots whenever he could. Many of the people, who had admired Kennedy, disliked the new president.

Johnson had entered politics during the Depression and strongly supported Franklin Roosevelt's New Deal. He cared deeply about America's poor. When Johnson became president 30 years later, poverty was not

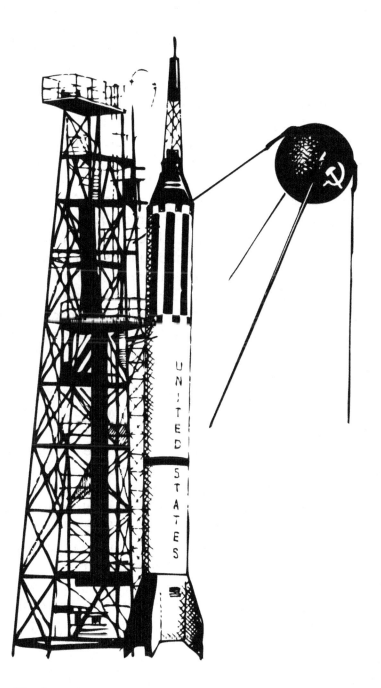

The Space Race—a U.S. Space Rocket and a Russian Spaceship

nearly as widespread, but millions of Americans were still poor. Johnson believed everyone should share in the wealth of a country as rich as the United States.

After he won the 1964 presidential election, Johnson created an anti-poverty plan he called The Great Society. Johnson hated the racism he had seen in Texas. It made him a strong civil rights advocate. His programs included job-training and money for decent housing. The Head Start program prepared young children from poor families for school. Some African-Americans were not sure they could trust Johnson, because he was the first Southern president in a century and African-Americans were still fighting for their rights in the South.

Johnson pushed for the passage of the Civil Rights Act of 1964, which made it illegal to discriminate against any person because of race, religion or the country your family came from. It became illegal for employers to discriminate when hiring employees. Labor unions could not discriminate against people who wanted to join. Hotels and restaurants had to serve everyone who could pay. The country took another step toward equal rights with the Voting Rights Act of 1965. It ended the tricks that kept many Southern blacks from voting. There were no black mayors in America in 1965, but by 1979, African-Americans were mayors in dozens of cities, including Atlanta, Detroit and Los Angeles.

The Civil Rights Act and the Voting Rights Act were important, but they did not end inequality. Some African-Americans were still angry at whites.

The Nation of Islam attracted African-Americans who were especially resentful about the discrimination against blacks. The Nation of Islam, sometimes called the Black Muslims, claimed to be followers of Islam but, in their version of Islam, blacks were superior to whites, and white people were "devils." This opposed the actual teachings of Islam, which say all races are equal. Black Muslims rejected integration and thought blacks should segregate themselves from whites. Many people joined the Nation of Islam after hearing the speeches of a brilliant young Black Muslim, Malcolm X, in the early 1960s.

Malcolm X was born in 1925 as Malcolm Little. He and other members of the Nation of Islam changed their last names to "X" to reject the "slave names" imposed on their ancestors, and to represent their unknown African ancestors.

Malcolm's father was a Christian minister who preached that blacks should be proud of their race. When Malcolm was only 6, his father was found dead, apparently murdered. At least one of his uncles was also lynched. By seventh grade, he was the only African-American in his class. He did very well in school and wanted to be a lawyer. The teacher had encouraged white children to pursue their dreams, but he told Malcolm that practicing law was not a realistic goal for blacks. He **suggested** carpentry.

Malcolm dropped out of school in the eighth grade, and pulled away from whites. Malcolm moved to Boston, then to Harlem. He drifted into gambling, bootlegging and selling and using drugs. After he moved back to Boston, he committed robberies in order to buy drugs, but was caught and sent to prison. He kicked his drug habit while in prison. He decided to read every book in the library there, and tried to pick up where his education had stopped. He also became a follower of the Nation of Islam.

Malcolm followed the strict Nation of Islam code of conduct and spread Black Muslim beliefs after he left prison. He was a powerful speaker, and soon millions of Americans heard his call for change "by any means necessary," (even violence) on radio and television.

The Symbols of the Nation of Islam

In 1964, Malcolm X made a pilgrimage to Mecca, the holy city of Islam. He discovered people of all colors united in their faith. When he returned to the United States, he still urged African-Americans to fight for their rights, but he no longer condemned all white people.

Malcolm X was murdered in 1965, before he could develop his new message that not all white people are racists. He left behind a powerful book about his life, *The Autobiography of Malcolm X*. Three black members of the Nation of Islam who still considered whites "devils" were **convicted** of killing Malcolm X.

The Civil Rights Movement was becoming divided. Like Malcolm X, some young blacks thought equality was not coming quickly enough. They began to reject integration, and talked about "black power." Some thought "black power" meant blacks should control their own communities. Others thought blacks should start a violent revolution against whites. Between 1964 and 1968, more than 100 race riots broke out in major U.S. cities, including Detroit and Los Angeles.

Martin Luther King Jr. was disturbed by the violence. He urged African-Americans to change society peacefully, and to ally themselves with nonracist whites. King led peaceful protests all over the country. He knew it was risky. Several civil rights workers were murdered in the early 1960s, and for years King thought he might also be murdered. In April 1968, in Memphis, Tennessee, King demonstrated for equal pay for black workers. The next day he was assassinated when he left his motel room for dinner. A white man was convicted of killing King.

The Civil Rights Movement was born of a **legacy** of slavery, but the struggle grew to include people of many races: Native Americans, Asian Americans, Hispanic Americans and many others.

The Holy Pilgrimage of Islam

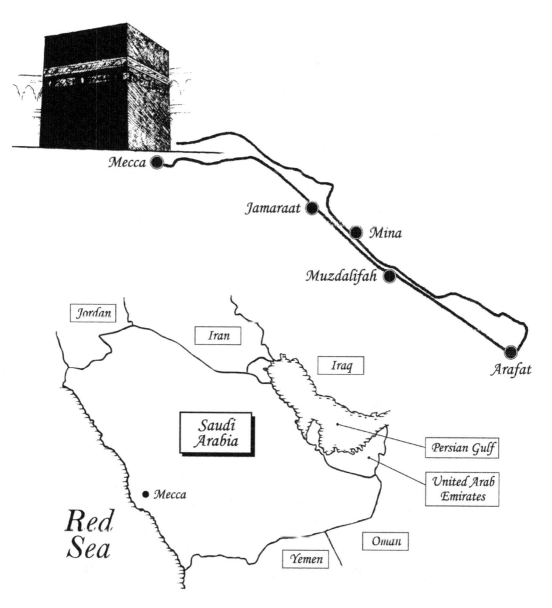

Mecca

Jamaraat

Mina

Muzdalifah

Arafat

Jordan

Iran

Iraq

Saudi Arabia

Persian Gulf

United Arab Emirates

Mecca

Oman

Yemen

Red Sea

Great Changes

The largest minority group in California and the southwestern states in the 1960s was Mexican Americans. For more than 100 years, Mexican Americans had suffered many of the same injustices as African-Americans in the South. They were forced into segregated schools and not allowed in hotels or restaurants. Mexican Americans were often forced to take the hardest, dirtiest, lowest-paid jobs. Many became poor, migrant farm workers who could only hope for temporary work. They were paid so little that they had to live in overcrowded labor camps.

One Mexican American, Cesar Chavez, led the movement to improve the lives of migrant workers. Chavez came from a family of poor migrants. He formed the United Farm Workers union in the early 1960s and fought for higher migrant-worker pay and better living conditions.

Some California farmers who grew grapes were especially unfair to the workers. The union called a strike against the grape growers in 1965 that lasted for years. Some of the farmers eventually agreed to raise the pay and living standards of their workers, but others refused. In 1967, Chavez asked

Migrant Farm Workers in the Fields in California

Americans to boycott grapes. All over the country, people refused to buy grapes to support the migrant workers. In 1970, the rest of the growers gave in and signed agreements with the union.

The Civil Rights Movement encouraged American Indians to demand better treatment and policies, too.

A mid-1940s government policy called "termination" overturned much of John Collier's Indian New Deal, which had provided programs and financial support for Native Americans. It was another way to assimilate Native Americans into American society. This program eliminated tribal **autonomy**, and made tribes follow state laws and pay taxes. It required the shared property of the tribe to be divided among individual members. This action broke one of the biggest bonds that held the tribes together. The government also began to relocate Indians from reservations to urban areas, thus breaking these tribal bonds even more. Termination saved the government money, but it also threatened the Native American way of life. Between 1954 and 1966, the federal government terminated more than 100 tribes.

Native American civil rights activists began to draw attention to Native Americans suffering. Tribes demanded that they be involved in the design and control of programs that **affected** them. Eventually, the government renewed economic aid, and adopted a new policy of "self-determination." President Lyndon Johnson explained in 1968 that this new policy gave Native Americans "an opportunity to remain in their homelands, if they choose, without surrendering their dignity; an opportunity to move to the towns and cities of America, if they choose, equipped with the skills to live in equality and dignity." President Richard Nixon affirmed that policy in 1970. Self-determination restored federal financial support and gave tribes control of their land and themselves.

Native Americans who live on reservations today can choose their own government. States are not allowed to regulate how Indians live on reservations, or how they use reservation lands. A state cannot tax Indians who live on reservations. If they live off the reservation, Native Americans must pay the same taxes and obey the same laws as everyone else. Since Native Americans must obey U.S. laws when off the reservation, non-Indians must obey tribal laws and customs when on the reservation.

The United States joined a war in Southeast Asia in the early 1960s that became the longest war in our history. The Vietnam War was a bloody and frustrating conflict that sharply divided Americans.

Vietnam was a French colony until the French withdrew in 1954. This left Vietnam divided into two countries—a communist north and a non-communist south. The North Vietnamese tried to overthrow the South

Vietnamese government by arming and training communist guerillas. "Guerillas" are fighters who are not part of a regular army. They move quickly because they usually fight in small groups, and they do not wear uniforms.

President Kennedy sent thousands of American soldiers to South Vietnam to "advise" South Vietnamese troops. The communist guerillas, called the Viet Cong, (who appeared in early 1965) seemed to be gaining ground in their attempt to overthrow the South Vietnamese government.

President Johnson feared a South Vietnamese defeat might open the way for communist China to dominate all of eastern Asia, just as the Soviet Union dominated Eastern Europe. He did not want that to happen. Johnson sent 200,000 more American troops and also sent the U.S. Air Force to bomb North Vietnam.

Just as in the Civil War, most Americans believed that the war would be over in a few weeks. Instead, the bombing made the Viet Cong more determined. The United States increased the bombing and sent more troops. Thousands of Americans were killed, but Americans killed even more Viet Cong. The Viet Cong and the North Vietnamese were dedicated soldiers fighting for their country. Communist leaders told their followers that Americans wanted to colonize Vietnam.

As Americans died in Vietnam, bitter arguments arose between American "hawks," who thought the United States should keep fighting, and "doves," who wanted the troops to come home. Hawks argued that the U.S. was protecting a small, weak country from communism. Doves argued that the U.S. shouldn't have **interfered** in a civil war.

On college campuses, anti-war feelings were especially strong. Many draft-age students thought that the money spent on the war should be used to fight poverty and racism at home. Anti-war demonstrations broke out at colleges across the country, sometimes turning violent.

During demonstrations at Kent State University in Ohio in 1970, the National Guard (part-time citizen-soldiers) was called out. Students started throwing rocks at the guardsmen. The soldiers were in no real danger, but had little experience with this kind of **confrontation**. As a result, several of the armed guardsmen panicked, and fired into the crowd. Fifteen students were shot, and four died. The shootings shocked the country and turned even more people against the war.

By the late 1960s, college students weren't the only rebels, and war wasn't the only issue. Teenagers and young adults began behaving very differently from their elders. Young people on one side of the "generation gap" used language that parents, on the other side of the gap, did not understand. The young people listened to a new kind of music—rock 'n'

The Vietnam War
1956-1975

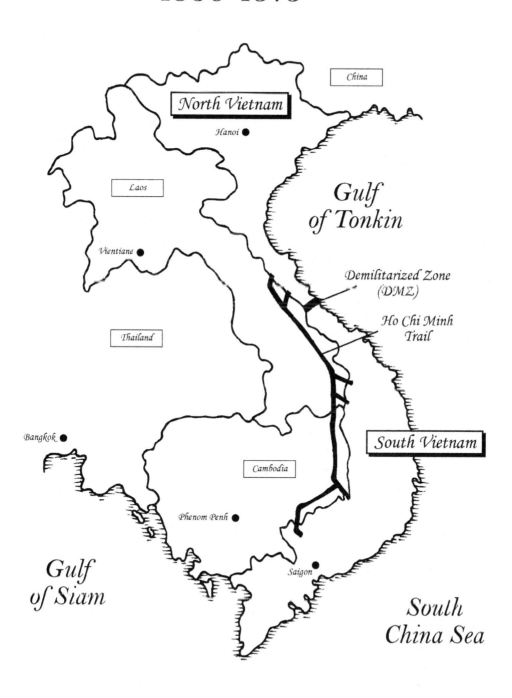

China

North Vietnam

Hanoi ●

Laos

Gulf
of Tonkin

Vientiane ●

Demilitarized Zone
(DMZ)

Ho Chi Minh
Trail

Thailand

Bangkok ●

Cambodia

South Vietnam

Phenom Penh ●

Gulf
of Siam

Saigon ●

South
China Sea

roll—that parents considered too loud and weird. They called things they liked "groovy," and called everyone, even girls, "man."

Young Americans had also rebelled during the Roaring Twenties, but the 1960s rebellion was more extreme. Many young people only wanted to enjoy themselves, but others questioned basic American values.

One group of young people wanted their own society, one based on love and peace. They felt that America was a **greedy, materialistic,** warlike nation. These young people left their schools and jobs and gathered in major cities, like San Francisco and New York. They became known as "hippies," because they were "hip," or cool, or they called themselves "flower children," because they handed out flowers as a sign of peace and friendship. Many hippies wore beads and headbands; men and women both wore long, straight hair, and men often grew beards. Women wore new "mini-skirts" high above their knees.

The youth movement peaked in August 1969, when 400,000 young people gathered on a farm in Woodstock, New York for a rock music festival. For three days, hundreds of thousands of people listened to rock music, danced, talked and enjoyed each other's company. Police were amazed that such a huge crowd was also so peaceful. It was a hippie dream—a world of friendship and peace.

Unfortunately, there was a dark side to the youth movement. Many teens that were too young to take care of themselves ran away from home and often became addicted to illegal drugs or died of **overdoses**.

The month before Woodstock, President Kennedy's dream of reaching the moon before 1970 was realized. Astronauts Michael Collins, Buzz Aldrin and Neil Armstrong, lifted off from Cape Canaveral (later renamed Cape Kennedy), Florida in July 1969. Their spaceship was called the *Columbia*, after Christopher Columbus. Just four days later, on July 20, the *Columbia* went into orbit around the moon. Aldrin and Armstrong, in a smaller craft called the *Eagle*, left the *Columbia* and flew down to the Sea of Tranquility—a dry, smooth area on the moon. At 4:17 p.m. Eastern time, Neil Armstrong changed history.

"Houston, Tranquility Base here. The *Eagle* has landed," Armstrong radioed back to Earth.

Armstrong left the *Eagle* first. As he took the last step from the ladder to the moon's dusty surface, he famously said, "That's one small step for a man, one giant leap for mankind."

A television camera on the spacecraft transmitted pictures of the moment to half a billion people across the world. The astronauts of the Apollo 11 mission planted an American flag that was held up with a pole, so that it appeared to "fly" on the airless, windless moon.

These men were not claiming the moon for the United States. They had made the dangerous journey just to add to man's knowledge of the universe. The moon would be open to any nation—the flag was just a symbol that the astronauts had been there. The astronauts also left behind a small steel sign.

"Here men from Planet Earth first set foot on the Moon July 1969. We came in peace for all mankind," it read.

American Astronaut Walking on the Moon

Richard M. Nixon promised to end the war in Vietnam when he became president in 1969. He did bring some soldiers home, but he also increased bombing in North Vietnam. Nixon had hoped the bombing would force the North Vietnamese to surrender.

In January 1973, the two sides finally signed a **cease-fire** that forced Americans to leave the country. The last American troops came home two months later, ending the conflict (Congress never officially declared war on Vietnam). This conflict had lasted longer than any in American history (through the administrations of five presidents).

South Vietnam battled for two more years, but finally surrendered in April 1975, when the North Vietnamese captured the South's capital, Saigon. The two Vietnams became the Socialist Republic of Vietnam.

The American government faced its second-greatest crisis when President Nixon became the first president to be forced to resign from office in **disgrace**.

Five men were arrested in Washington, D.C. for breaking into a Democratic Party office in the Watergate office complex during the 1972 presidential campaign. The burglars were looking for embarrassing information about the Democratic **candidate**.

At first, police and the public didn't see any connection between the burglars and Nixon's campaign. In November 1972, Nixon was reelected. Then, reporters from The Washington Post newspaper learned that the burglars had committed other illegal break-ins against Democrats. Also, the president might have supported the crimes. It's still unknown if Nixon was behind the break-ins, but he did try to stop the investigation, which is a serious crime.

The House of Representatives wrote articles of impeachment, or charges, against the president after a two-year Congressional investigation. (Only the House can impeach, or charge, a president with serious wrongdoing. An impeached president is then tried in the Senate.) Nixon was charged with acting "in a manner contrary to his trust as President and **subversive** of constitutional government." Nixon denied committing any crime, but resigned in August 1974 to avoid impeachment. Vice President Gerald R. Ford became president.

Many people stopped trusting the American government after "Watergate." Others said the fact that Nixon was forced from office, and that another president took over without violence, proved that the American system works. It proved the United States is "a government of laws, not of men," a government in which no one, not even the president, is above the law.

A Watergate Burglar

President Ford **pardoned** Nixon. He did not want the former president charged with any crimes. He believed that the nation would not be able to leave these problems behind if the government had to conduct a lengthy criminal trial.

The feminist movement resurged in the 1960s and 1970s. "Feminists" believe in equal rights and opportunities for women. After women won the right to vote in 1920, many people thought that women had achieved equal standing with men. Women, however, still could not become soldiers, mechanics, doctors, artists or any of a hundred other things. They were still supposed to marry and raise children.

In 1963, Betty Friedan published *The Feminine Mystique*. (A "mystique" is a false way of thinking or feeling.) Friedan wrote that the "housewife trap" made American women unhappy, because women could not act independently of men to develop their talents and interests.

When women did work outside the home, Friedan and other feminists complained that women were only allowed to work in "women's jobs," like nursing and teaching. Even when a woman did get a "man's" job, she was usually paid less than men who did the same work. "Women's liberation" gained momentum. Friedan and other feminists founded NOW—the National Organization for Women—in 1966. They wanted equality with men *now*. NOW also called for a constitutional amendment that would say that, "equality of rights under the law shall not be denied or abridged by the United States or by any State on account of sex."

The Equal Rights Amendment (ERA) passed both houses of Congress in 1972. After Congress passes an amendment, it must to be approved by 75 percent of the states. More than half the states ratified the ERA within a year. However, ERA supporters never got the majority they needed. Some people, even some women, said the Civil Rights Act of 1964 had already established equality for women when it prohibited discrimination based on race, religion, national origin *and gender*. The ERA was never passed.

Still, the number of women doctors more than doubled in the 1970s, and the number of women lawyers tripled. United States military academies opened to women students for the first time in 1976. Now women can be scientists, construction workers, writers, farmers, police officers, astronauts, governors and senators. Many women still choose to be homemakers, but now it is a choice, not their only option.

The United States celebrated its **bicentennial** or 200th birthday, on July 4, 1976. Many people visited Philadelphia, where the *Declaration of Independence* was signed on July 4, 1776. British Queen Elizabeth II, the great-great-great-great granddaughter of King George III, was one of the visitors.

Opening of More Career Fields for Women

At 2 p.m. the Liberty Bell—which was fragile since it cracked years earlier—was struck softly with a **rubber mallet** to celebrate. At the same moment, church bells rang all over the nation, celebrating the "Great Experiment" in democracy.

In New York City, millions of people watched more than 200 ships from more than 30 nations sail into New York Harbor and up the Hudson River. Many of these were impressive, "tall ships" like those that existed during the Revolutionary War. These beautiful sailing ships reminded Americans, immigrants, and the world of the difficult voyages to the place, the idea, called America.

Jimmy Carter, calling himself "the people's president" was elected president later that year. He and First Lady Rosalynn Carter walked down Pennsylvania Avenue after his inauguration, rather than travel as passengers in a limousine.

He was not very successful in managing the U.S. economy, but Carter did convince Israel and Egypt, which had been at war for five years, to sign a historic peace treaty.

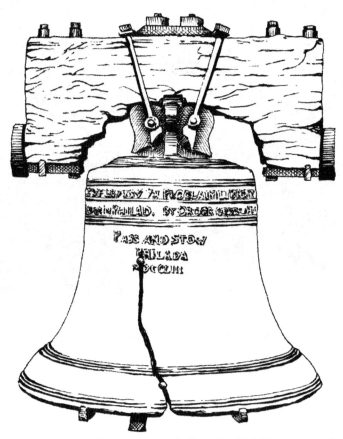

The Ringing of the Liberty Bell at the U.S. Bicentennial

The Changing World 1992-2008

Triumph of Self-Government

America continued to change. During an energy shortage in the 1970s, people started moving from the manufacturing areas in the North and Northeast to the warmer South and Southwest. The migration altered the composition of the House of Representatives and the balance of power.

The invention of personal computers in the 1970s also started changing the way Americans lived and did business. The Department of Defense created the Internet as an experiment, but by 2000 more than 500 million people worldwide were connected. Instant communication between people and companies on the Internet and on new wireless telephones created new jobs and destroyed old ones.

Multi-national companies grew rapidly. Manufacturing globalized—production could occur in several countries—so that the product could be made by the cheapest labor. This **globalization**, however, cost many Americans their jobs.

Latin American and Asian immigration began to increase in the 1980s. By 2012, Hispanics replaced blacks as the largest minority. Asians were the third largest group of immigrants. Thanks largely to immigration, the population broke the 300-million mark in 2000—an increase of more than 10 percent in just 10 years. New Americans often settled in the South and Southwest, which caused an additional shift in political boundaries and representation. The rights of immigrants and minorities became more important than ever in politics.

By 1980, many Americans thought the federal government was too big, too restrictive, and taxes were too high. Republican Ronald Reagan promised to downsize government and spending, and defeated President Jimmy Carter in the presidential election.

Reagan was the governor of California, a former movie star and the oldest person to be elected president. He convinced members of both political parties to pass laws that improved the economy, including a big tax cut. He also reduced some of the government's power to make the rules for big companies.

President Reagan scored a major success in 1987 when the Soviet Union and the United States agreed to eliminate many nuclear weapons in Europe. President Reagan also pressured Soviet leader Mikhail Gorbachev to remove the Berlin Wall, and increase freedom in Eastern Europe. Gorbachev tore the wall down in 1989. The Cold War was finally over.

Reagan's successor, George H. Bush, sent American troops to the Middle East in 1990. He authorized Operation Desert Storm after Iraq invaded Kuwait to grab Kuwait's oil wells. By February 1991, the Persian Gulf War (Operation Desert Storm) was over, and Kuwait was independent again.

In 1992, Bill Clinton was elected president after he promised to reverse the economic **recession**. Congress passed the North American Free Trade Agreement (NAFTA), which created a free-trade zone with Canada and Mexico. The economy improved. This led to a rare federal budget surplus in 1998, which allowed Congress to pay off some of the debts the U.S. owed. Clinton was popular then, but his second term was full of **scandal**. His behavior with a young female staffer led to his impeachment in 1998. Though he was charged, the Senate acquitted him, and he completed his second term.

The explosive growth of the Internet in the 1990s made most people and business **dependent** on computers for communication and daily business. New Year's Eve, 1999, marked the end of the **millennium**. Many people were afraid the change to the year 2000 would **crash** computers all over the world. Companies spent billions of dollars to avoid problems, but nothing bad happened.

George W. Bush, son of George H. Bush, won the closest presidential election in history in November 2000. Less than eight months after he took office, on September 11, 2001 terrorists from the Middle East hijacked four airplanes. Two flew into the two World Trade Center towers in New York City and another crashed into the Pentagon in Washington, D.C. The last plane, which the hijackers probably planned to use to destroy the U.S.

Capitol building (where Congress meets), crashed in a field in Pennsylvania because the passengers attacked the hijackers.

The American sense of security was damaged. More than 3,000 Americans died in the attacks. The terrorists were members of a terrorist group called al-Qaida, which considers the United States evil.

The Destruction of the World Trade Center in New York

President Bush created the Department of Homeland Security in response to the attacks. This department manages security at American airports, train stations and seaports. It also responds to disasters like hurricanes, tornados and floods.

Bush also sent American armed forces who joined with U.N. troops to invade Iraq in 2003. He thought Iraq was developing nuclear weapons and had helped the terrorists who attacked the United States on 9/11. This war, like the Civil War and the Vietnam War, was supposed to end quickly. Instead, it lasted years, and led to new terror attacks. It also established that Iraq had *not* had any "weapons of mass destruction."

Hurricane Katrina, the deadliest natural disaster in U.S. history, hit New Orleans, Louisiana on August 29, 2005. At least 1,800 people died in the hurricane and the flooding that followed. A system of **levees** that was supposed to protect the city failed. President Bush and Homeland Security were criticized for taking days to get drinking water to the area, and years to get some people into new homes.

The economy was failing again. The technology boom from increased use of the Internet fell apart. The government spent billions of dollars on the war in the Middle East. At the same time, the banking and real estate markets were falsely making people think the economy was growing. Many people bought houses they couldn't afford because banks lent them more money than they could pay back. Many people lost their jobs when Internet companies started going bankrupt. Just as in 1929, this created many more economic problems.

In 2008, Democratic presidential candidate Barack Obama, just like Franklin Roosevelt, promised to energize the economy. He also promised to bring the troops home from the Middle East. Obama was an inspiring speaker, and many people believed it was time for a change. His election was a major **milestone** in United States history because Obama became the first black president.

Many American children have been told that anyone could become president, that everyone is equal, and that individual effort makes the difference in achieving a dream. With Obama's victory, Martin Luther King Jr.'s dream was finally fulfilled—people are now elected because of their character, not the color of their skin.

President Barack Obama at his Inauguration in 2008 and Martin
Luther King Jr at his Speech in Washington, D.C. in 1963

Appendix A

Study Questions For Each Section

NOTE: Asterisk * means possible state test question.

Coming to America

Write a sentence explaining the importance of each term or name:

Paul Revere	Mayflower	Thomas Paine
Puritans	Benjamin Franklin	Pilgrims
Jamestown	Boston Tea Party	Slavery

1. What is <u>one</u> reason European colonists came to America?
2. Who lived in America before the Europeans arrived?
3. What ocean is on the East Coast of the United States?
4. What group of people were taken to America and sold as slaves?
*5. How were the goals of the Jamestown colonists of Virginia different from the goals of the Puritan colonists of Massachusetts?

Fight For Self Government

Write a sentence explaining the importance of each term or name:

George Washington	Redcoats	Benedict Arnold
Yankee Doodle	Militia	Delegate
Marquis de Lafayette	Hessians	Second Continental Congress

1. There were 13 original states. Name <u>three.</u>
2. Who wrote the Declaration of Independence and when was it adopted?
3. What are <u>two</u> rights in the Declaration of Independence?
4. Why does the flag have 13 stripes?

Becoming The United States

Write a sentence explaining the importance of each term or name:

Amendment	Bill of Rights
Articles of Confederation	Federalist Papers
Checks and Balances	Veto

1.   What were some of the problems with the government set up by the Articles of Confederation?
2.   When was the Constitution written and what does it do?
3.   Why did the framers (writers) of the Constitution make it so difficult to amend the Constitution?
4.   The idea of self-government is in the first three words of the Constitution. What are these words?
5.   How many amendments does the Constitution have today?
6.   Name one branch or part of the government.
7.   What are the two parts of the U.S. Congress?
8.   What is the highest court in the United States?
9.   A president is elected for how many years?
10.   Under the Constitution, some powers belong to the federal government. What is one power of the federal government?
11.   Why do some states have more Representatives than other states?
12.   Who makes federal laws?
13.   What is one responsibility that is only for United States citizens?
14.   What are the natural rights given to all Americans?
15.   What are two rights of everyone living in the United States?
16.   What does the judicial branch do?
17.   How many justices are on the Supreme Court?
*18.   How do you define the 'right of privacy?'
*19.   Why is it important for the commander-in-chief to be civilian rather than a military general?

First Government

Write a sentence explaining the importance of each term or name:

Sacajawea	Meriwether Lewis	Louisiana Purchase
Francis Scott Key	John Adams	War of 1812
Fort	Alexander Hamilton	Capitol

1.   What is the name of the national anthem?
2.   What is the capital of the United States?
3.   What ocean is on the West Coast of the United States?
4.   Name <u>one</u> of the two longest rivers in the United States.
5.   What does the President's Cabinet do? Name 2 positions.

First Expansion of The United States

Write a sentence explaining the importance of each term or name:

Monroe Doctrine   Self-made Man   Trail of Tears
Seminole   Impeachment   Prairie Schooner
Oregon Trail   Santé Fe Trail   General Santa Ana
Andrew Jackson

1.   How did the Louisiana Purchase affect the United States?
2.   Between 1830 and 1850, the United States increased by one third.
      Most of the land was acquired by: (choose one and explain)
            a. War   c. Rebellion
            b. Purchase   d. Exchange
*3.   Why was the concept of 'manifest destiny' so appealing to the
      Americans in the 1840s?

Reform in The United States

Write a sentence explaining the importance of each term or name:

Frederick Douglass   Abolitionist   Elizabeth Cady Stanton
Dorothea Dix   Horace Mann   Seneca Fall Convention
Susan B. Anthony   Temperance Movement

1.   What is universal education?
2.   Who founded the National Woman Suffrage Association?
*3.   What was the Homestead Act and why was it so important?

A Nation Divided

Write a sentence explaining the importance of each term or name:

Ulysses S. Grant   Robert E. Lee   Emancipation Proclamation
Gettysburg Address Dred Scott   Appomattox Court House
Confederacy   Jefferson Davis   Underground Railroad
Secession   Harriet Tubman   Uncle Tom's Cabin
William Tecumseh Sherman

1.   Name <u>one</u> problem that led to the Civil War.
*2.   What is the main effect of the Missouri Compromise?
3.   Name the U.S. war between the North and the South.
4.   What was one important thing that Abraham Lincoln did?
5.   What did the Emancipation Proclamation do?
*6.   Who do you think had the greatest impact on American history about opposing slavery and why?
        John Brown, Harriet Beecher Stowe, Harriet Tubman.
*7.   Using the American Revolution, the creation of the Constitution, and the Civil War as major examples: write about how the American political society changed the roles of important individuals who supported the change.
        Include:
        a)   The rule of law, inalienable rights, equality, and limited government.
        b)   The development of governmental roles in American life.
        c)   The competing opinions on the responsibilities of governments (federal and state).
        d)   The development of political parties.
        e)   America's political and economic role in the world.

Reunification and Growth

Write a sentence explaining the significance of each term or name:

Carpetbagger   Scalawag   John Wilkes Booth
Ku Klux Klan   Poll tax   Freedmen's Bureau
14th Amendment   15th Amendment   Reconstruction

1.   What effect did the war have on the economies of the North and the South?
2.   Why was President Johnson impeached? Why was this significant?

*3. Can you name another U.S. president who was impeached and for what reason?

*4. What were the Black Codes and what was their significance?

Second Expansion of The United States

Write a sentence explaining the importance of each term or name:

Gold Rush   Thomas Edison   Central Pacific Railroad
Homestead Act   Pony Express   Union Pacific Railroad
Sioux

*1. In what way did immigration and migration shape the early United States?

2. What invention do you think was most significant during this period? Explain your answer.

3. Name 3 major Native American tribes in the U.S.

*4. Describe the major changes in American life before 1877 including
   a) Changing political boundaries of the United States
   b) Changes in the size, location, and composition of the population
   c) Changes in trade, transportation, and communication

The Wild West

Write a sentence explaining the importance of each term or name:

Apache   Pueblo   Alexander Graham Bell
Sitting Bull   Little Big Horn Assimilation
Patent   Nez Perce   George Washington Carver

1. Name one U.S. Territory.

2. How successful were the government's efforts to promote settlement of the Great Plains? Give examples to support your answer.

*3. Why do you think the Dawes Act failed?

*4. Why did Native Americans resist assimilation?

*5. Where is the Statue of Liberty? What does it symbolize?

*6. Identify 3 differences between the culture of the North American Indians and the white settlers of the Great Plains.

Industrialization in The United States

Write a sentence explaining the significance of each term or name:

Capitalist	Monopoly	Andrew Carnegie
John D. Rockefeller	Trust	Strike
Populism	Labor Union	J.P. Morgan

1. Why did workers form unions in the late 19th century?
2. If the United States had been poor in natural resources, how would industrialization been affected?
*3. Analyze the factors that helped the United States to become a major industrial power, including
   a) Advantages of physical geography
   b) Increase in labor through immigration and migration
   c) Economic policies of government and industrial leaders
   d) Technological advances

Social Change

Write a sentence explaining the significance of each term or name:

Settlement House	Muckraker	NAACP
Puerto Rico	Philanthropist	Jane Addams
Booker T. Washington	Yellow journalism	USS Maine

1. Why was the Panama Canal important to the U.S.?
2. What would you do to improve the living conditions in the U.S. during this time?
3. How did the railroads benefit from and contribute to the industrialization of the U.S.?
4. What was the role of reform organizations, movements and individuals in promoting change, for example, settlement house movement, the National Association for the Advancement of Colored People, Jane Addams, W.E.B. Du Bois?
*5. Identify the core (main) ideas of American society as shown in the documents below and analyze the ways that American society moved toward and/or away from its core ideals.
   a) Declaration of Independence
   b) The U.S. Constitution
   c) Bill of Rights
   d) The Gettysburg Address
   e) 13th, 14th, and 15th Amendments

Moving Into the World

Write a sentence explaining the importance of each term or name:

Suffrage	Charlie Chaplin	Charles Lindbergh
League of Nations	Flapper	Communism
Amelia Earhart	Langston Hughes	Harlem
Renaissance	Creationism	Evolution
Eighteenth Amendment		

1. Name <u>one</u> war fought by the United States in the 1900s.
2. Explain the causes of World War I, the reasons for American neutrality and eventual entry into the war.
3. Who was President during World War I?
4. What new weapons made World War I more deadly than previous wars?
5. What were the effects of Prohibition?
*6. How did the changes in technology in the 1920s influence American life?
*7. Why were American **ties** with the Allies stronger than its ties with the Central Powers?

The Depression Years

Write a sentence explaining the importance of each term or name:

Hoover Dam	Great Depression	Civilian Conservation Corps
Stock	Deficit Spending	Indian Reorganization Act
New Deal		

1. Which areas were included in the Dust Bowl region?
2. What were some of the effects of the stock market crash of 1929?
3. List <u>five</u> New Deal agencies that are still around today.
*4. Explain and evaluate Roosevelt's New Deal Policies including:
   a) Expanding the federal government's responsibilities to protect the environment, for example, Dust Bowl and the Tennessee Valley, unemployment, needs of workers, farmers, poor, and elderly
   b) **Consequences** of New Deal policies, for example, promoting workers' rights, development of Social Security program, and banking and financial regulation, conservation practices, crop subsidies.

*5.   Do you think it would have been difficult for individuals to recover financially during the Depression without the entire economic recovery? Why or why not?

The War Years

Write a sentence explaining the importance of each term or name:

Rosie the Riveter	Nazi	Fascism
Blitzkrieg	Holocaust	Internment
Dwight Eisenhower	Genocide	Atomic Bomb
Winston Churchill	Axis Powers	Battle of Midway
Yalta		

1.   Why did the United States enter World War II?
2.   What was the significance of the Battle of Stalingrad?
3.   How did the United States use its resources to achieve victory?
4.   Why did Truman decide to use the A-bomb?
*5.   Would you support the use of nuclear weapons today? And if so, under what circumstances?
*6.   Analyze the changes in American life caused by U.S. participation in World War II:
        a)   Economic, military, and social resources used in the war
        b)   Role of women and minorities in the war effort
        c)   Internment of Japanese-Americans

Becoming a World Example

Write a sentence explaining the importance of each term or name:

Iron Curtain	NATO	Truman Doctrine
Marshall Plan	United Nations	McCarthyism
H-Bomb	Cold War	G.I.
Korea	Suburbs	

1.   Which of the superpowers contributed more to the Cold War during the 1950s?
2.   During the Cold War, what was the main concern of the United States?
3.   The arms race between the Soviet Union and the United States was as dangerous as a war. Do you agree or disagree? Why?

*4.   Analyze the factors that contributed to the Cold War including
    a)   Differences in political beliefs and values, and the economic
            and governmental institutions of the U.S. and U.S.S.R.
    b)   Actions by both countries in the last years of World War
            II and shortly afterward, for example, the use of the atomic
            bomb, the Marshall Plan, the Truman Doctrine, North
            American Treaty Alliance (NATO).

Civil Rights in Post WWII America

Write a sentence explaining the significance of each term or name:

NASA   Rosa Parks   Fidel Castro
Sputnik   Nation of Islam   Peace Corps
Berlin Wall   Great Society   Malcolm X
Martin Luther King, Jr.   Brown vs. the Board of Education

1.   What were the roots of Martin Luther King's beliefs about non-
        violent actions?
2.   Do you think the non-violence used by the civil rights activists was a
        good tactic? Why?
3.   What movement tried to end racial discrimination?
*4.   Compare the strategies of Martin Luther King and Malcolm X.
        Whose methods do you think were more effective? Explain.
5.   What was the most important result of the Cuban missile crisis?
6.   Do you agree with John F. Kennedy's view about the relationship
        between individuals and their country?
*7.   Analyze the key events, ideals, documents, and organizations in the
        struggle for civil rights by African Americans.
    a)   The impact of WWII, for example, racial integration of the
            military.
    b)   Supreme Court decisions and governmental actions, for
            example, Brown vs. Board (1954), Civil Rights Act (1957),
            Civil Rights Act (1964), Voting Rights Act (1965).
    c)   Protest movements, organizations, and civil actions, for
            example, Montgomery Bus Boycott (1955-1956), March on
            Washington (1963), National Association
            for the Advancement of Colored People (NAACP),
            Nation of Islam.

A Time of Great Changes

Write a sentence explaining the significance of each term or name:

Viet Cong   Watergate   Guerillas
Bicentennial   Cesar Chavez   Neil Armstrong
Self-determination   Betty Friedan   Draft
Feminism   NOW

*1.   In your opinion why didn't the hippies succeed?
2.   In what ways can a president misuse power?
*3.   What is the "rule of law"? Give an example from U.S. history.
*4.   Analyze the causes and course of the women's rights movement in
       the 1960s and 1970s including increasing number of women in the
       work force, National Organization for Women (NOW), and the
       Equal Rights Amendment (ERA).

The Changing World

Write a sentence explaining the significance of each term or name:

NAFTA   World Trade Center   Internet
Millennium   Multinational Corporation   Desert Storm
Department of Homeland Security

1.   What resources did the Internet make available?
2.   What were the factors that led to the end of the Cold War including
       policies of the U.S. and U.S.S.R. and their leaders, the political
       breakup of the Soviet Union?
3.   Analyze how the attacks on 9/11 and the response to terrorism
       have changed American domestic and international policies.
*4.   Explain the role of the United States as a super-power in the post-
       Cold War world, including advantages, disadvantages, and new
       challenges.
*5.   What are the important issues that affect the world today? Choose
       4 from the following list and explain (conservation, women at work,
       social security, terrorism, U.S. foreign policy, immigration, crime,
       education, communication, health care, poverty).

Appendix B

IN CONGRESS, July 4, 1776.

The unanimous Declaration of the thirteen United States of America,

When in the Course of human events, it becomes necessary for one people to dissolve the political bands which have connected them with another, and to assume among the powers of the earth, the separate and equal station to which the Laws of Nature and of Nature's God entitle them, a decent respect to the opinions of mankind requires that they should declare the causes which impel them to the separation.

We hold these truths to be self-evident, that all men are created equal, that they are endowed by their Creator with certain unalienable Rights, that among these are Life, Liberty and the pursuit of Happiness. That to secure these rights, Governments are instituted among Men, deriving their just powers from the consent of the governed, That whenever any Form of Government becomes destructive of these ends, it is the Right of the People to alter or to abolish it, and to institute new Government, laying its foundation on such principles and organizing its powers in such form, as to them shall seem most likely to effect their Safety and Happiness. Prudence, indeed, will dictate that Governments long established should not be changed for light and transient causes; and accordingly all experience hath shewn, that mankind are more disposed to suffer, while evils are sufferable, than to right themselves by abolishing the forms to which they are accustomed. But when a long train of abuses and usurpations, pursuing invariably the same Object evinces a design to reduce them under absolute Despotism, it is their right, it is their duty, to throw off such Government, and to provide new Guards for their future security. Such has been the patient sufferance of these Colonies; and such is now the necessity which constrains them to alter their former Systems of Government. The history of the present King of Great Britain is a history of repeated injuries and usurpations, all having in direct object the establishment of an absolute Tyranny over these States. To prove this, let Facts be submitted to a candid world.

He has refused his Assent to Laws, the most wholesome and necessary for the public good.

He has forbidden his Governors to pass Laws of immediate and pressing importance, unless suspended in their operation till his Assent should be obtained; and when so suspended, he has utterly neglected to attend to them.

He has refused to pass other Laws for the accommodation of large districts of people, unless those people would relinquish the right of Representation in the Legislature, a right inestimable to them and formidable to tyrants only.

He has called together legislative bodies at places unusual, uncomfortable, and distant from the depository of their public Records, for the sole purpose of fatiguing them into compliance with his measures.

He has dissolved Representative Houses repeatedly, for opposing with manly firmness his invasions on the rights of the people.

He has refused for a long time, after such dissolutions, to cause others to be elected; whereby the Legislative powers, incapable of Annihilation, have returned to the People at large for their exercise; the State remaining in the mean time exposed to all the dangers of invasion from without, and convulsions within.

He has endeavoured to prevent the population of these States; for that purpose obstructing the Laws for Naturalization of Foreigners; refusing to pass others to encourage their migrations hither, and raising the conditions of new Appropriations of Lands.

He has obstructed the Administration of Justice, by refusing his Assent to Laws for establishing Judiciary powers.

He has made Judges dependent on his Will alone, for the tenure of their offices, and the amount and payment of their salaries.

He has erected a multitude of New Offices, and sent hither swarms of Officers to harass our people, and eat out their substance.

He has kept among us, in times of peace, Standing Armies without the Consent of our legislatures.

He has affected to render the Military independent of and superior to the Civil power.

He has combined with others to subject us to a jurisdiction foreign to our constitution, and unacknowledged by our laws; giving his Assent to their Acts of pretended Legislation:

For Quartering large bodies of armed troops among us:

For protecting them, by a mock Trial, from punishment for any Murders which they should commit on the Inhabitants of these States:

For cutting off our Trade with all parts of the world:

For imposing Taxes on us without our Consent:

For depriving us in many cases, of the benefits of Trial by Jury:

For transporting us beyond Seas to be tried for pretended offences

For abolishing the free System of English Laws in a neighbouring Province, establishing therein an Arbitrary government, and enlarging its Boundaries so as to render it at once an example and fit instrument for introducing the same absolute rule into these Colonies:

For taking away our Charters, abolishing our most valuable Laws, and altering fundamentally the Forms of our Governments:

For suspending our own Legislatures, and declaring themselves invested with power to legislate for us in all cases whatsoever.

He has abdicated Government here, by declaring us out of his Protection and waging War against us.

He has plundered our seas, ravaged our Coasts, burnt our towns, and destroyed the lives of our people.

He is at this time transporting large Armies of foreign Mercenaries to compleat the works of death, desolation and tyranny, already begun with circumstances of Cruelty & perfidy scarcely paralleled in the most barbarous ages, and totally unworthy the Head of a civilized nation.

He has constrained our fellow Citizens taken Captive on the high Seas to bear Arms against their Country, to become the executioners of their friends and Brethren, or to fall themselves by their Hands.

He has excited domestic insurrections amongst us, and has endeavoured to bring on the inhabitants of our frontiers, the merciless Indian Savages, whose known rule of warfare, is an undistinguished destruction of all ages, sexes and conditions.

In every stage of these Oppressions We have Petitioned for Redress in the most humble terms: Our repeated Petitions have been answered only by repeated injury. A Prince whose character is thus marked by every act which may define a Tyrant, is unfit to be the ruler of a free people.

Nor have We been wanting in attentions to our British brethren. We have warned them from time to time of attempts by their legislature to extend an unwarrantable jurisdiction over us. We have reminded them of the circumstances of our emigration and settlement here. We have appealed to their native justice and magnanimity, and we have conjured them by the ties of our common kindred to disavow these usurpations, which, would inevitably interrupt our connections and correspondence. They too have been deaf to the voice of justice and of consanguinity. We must, therefore, acquiesce in the necessity, which denounces our Separation, and hold them, as we hold the rest of mankind, Enemies in War, in Peace Friends.

We, therefore, the Representatives of the united States of America, in General Congress, Assembled, appealing to the Supreme Judge of the world for the rectitude of our intentions, do, in the Name, and by Authority of the good People of these Colonies, solemnly publish and declare, That these United Colonies are, and of Right ought to be Free and Independent States; that they are Absolved from all Allegiance to the British Crown, and that all political connection between them and the State of Great Britain, is and ought to be totally dissolved; and that as Free and Independent States, they have full Power to levy War, conclude Peace, contract Alliances, establish Commerce, and to do all other Acts and Things which Independent States may of right do. And for the support of this Declaration, with a firm reliance on the protection of divine Providence, we mutually pledge to each other our Lives, our Fortunes and our sacred Honor.

Appendix C

The Constitution of the United States (abridged)

Preamble

We the People of the United States, in Order to form a more perfect Union, establish Justice, insure domestic Tranquility, provide for the common defense, promote the general Welfare, and secure the Blessings of Liberty to ourselves and our Posterity, do ordain and establish this Constitution for the United States of America.

Summary of the Articles of the Constitution

Article I

Lists rules for forming and running Congress, the law-making branch of government. Divides Congress into two houses, the Senate and the House of Representatives, and describes the duties of each house. Lists the powers of the federal government.

Article II

Calls for a President to carry out the nation's laws. Describes procedures for electing the President and lists the President's powers.

Article III

Establishes a Supreme Court. Defines, and sets out laws for dealing with, treason against the United States.

Article IV

Forbids any state from treating a citizen of another state differently from its own citizens. Gives Congress the power to admit new states to the Union.

Article V

Lists steps for amending (adding to or changing) the Constitution. Changes approved by at least three-fourths of the states become law.

Article VI

Makes the new Constitution the supreme law of the land, and requires all Federal and state officials to support it.

Article VII

Establishes that if at least nine states ratify the Constitution of 1787, it is considered the law of the land.

Appendix D

Summary of the Amendments to the Constitution (abridged)
The first ten amendments make up the Bill of Rights, adopted in 1791.

Amendment I Guarantees freedom of religion, of speech, and of the press. Gives the people the right to meet peaceably and the right to voice complaints to the government.

Amendment II Says that states need to have groups of people ready to protect themselves, so therefore, people can own guns.

Amendment III Says the government cannot force you to let soldiers stay in your home during peacetime.

Amendment IV Guarantees the right to privacy. Says the government needs a good reason to think you broke the law before it can search you or your house or take away your belongings.

Amendment V Says the government must follow certain rules when it accuses someone of a crime. Forbids punishment without a trial. Guarantees **compensation** if property is taken by the government for public use.

Amendment VI Guarantees the right for people accused of crimes to a speedy, fair trial by jury.

Amendment VII Says if two people go to court to settle a disagreement, they can have a jury trial if the value is more than twenty dollars.

Amendment VIII Says people accused of crimes have a chance to get out of jail before trial.

Amendment IX The people hold more rights than only those listed in the Constitution.

Amendment X Says the states have all powers that the Constitution does not either give to the U.S. government or take away from the states.

Amendment XI (1789) Keeps any one of the states from being sued by citizens of another state or of a foreign country.

XII (1804) Establishes presidential election procedures.

XIII (1865) Forbids laws that unfairly deny citizens' rights and guarantees equal protection under the law to all.

XIV (1868) Defines national citizenship and requires states to provide all persons with equal protection of the laws.

XV (1870) Forbids depriving citizens of the right to vote because of race or color.

XVI (1913) Authorizes an income tax.

XVII (1913) Calls for senators to be elected by direct vote of the people.

XVIII (1919) The Prohibition Amendment. Forbids the manufacture or sale of liquor.

XIX (1920) Grants women the right to vote.

XX (1933) Starts presidential and congressional terms in January.

XXI (1933) Repeals the Eighteenth Amendment.

XXII (1951) Bars any President from serving more than two terms (eight years).

XXIII (1961) Gives residents of the District of Colombia (Washington, D.C.) the right to vote for President.

XXIV (1964) It is illegal to have as a voting requirement that one must pay taxes.

XXV (1967) Establishes rules for succession if a President cannot complete the term.

XXVI (1971) Lowers the legal voting age to eighteen.

XXVII (1992) Congressional salaries can't be changed until after the election of representatives.

Appendix E

New Colossus

Not like the brazen giant of Greek fame,
With conquering limbs astride from land to land;
Here at our sea-washed, sunset gates shall stand
A mighty woman with a torch, whose flame
Is the imprisoned lightning, and her name
Mother of Exiles. From her beacon-hand
Glows world-wide welcome; her mild eyes command
The air-bridged harbor that twin cities frame.
"Keep, ancient lands, your storied pomp!" cries she
With silent lips. "Give me your tired, your poor,
Your huddled masses yearning to breathe free,
The wretched refuse of your teeming shore.
Send these, the homeless, tempest-tost to me,
I lift my lamp beside the golden door!"

Emma Lazarus – Author
(inscribed on the base of the Statue of Liberty)

Appendix F

List of American Authors

Years	Name	Biography
1783-1859	Washington Irving	One of the earliest American fiction writers, New York City-born Irving wrote the famous tales *Rip Van Winkle* (published in 1819) and *The Legend of Sleepy Hollow* (published in 1820). Visit museumofwashingtonirving.com
1789-1851	James Fennimore Cooper	Cooper, who grew up in Cooperstown, N.Y., is best known for his five-book Leatherstocking series, including *The Last of the Mohicans*, first published in 1826. In his frontier tales, Cooper introduces the first American hero, Natty Bumppo, a white child raised by Delaware Indians who grows up into an adventurous, honorable and fearless woodsman. Visit http://external.oneonta.edu/cooper/
1803-1882	Ralph Waldo Emerson	Boston-born Emerson was an ordained minister, philosopher, essayist and poet whose writings explored the mind of man and his relationship with nature. Emerson's uniquely American vision and writing style is illustrated in the 1836 essay *Nature* and the 1841 essay *Self-Reliance*. Visit rwe.org

1804-1864	Nathaniel Hawthorne	The Salem Massachusetts-born Hawthorne is known for his stories about sin, guilt and witchcraft in Puritan New England. His 1850 masterpiece was *The Scarlet Letter* and the 1851 classic *The House of Seven Gables*. Visit hawthorneassoc.com
1809-1949	Edgar Allan Poe	Boston-born Poe was a literary critic in his time and may have been the nation's first published horror, mystery and science fiction writer. Poe wrote eerie and mysterious tales such as his 1843 short story "The Tell-Tale Heart" and 1845 poem "The Raven". Visit eapoe.org or poestories.com
1817-1862	Henry David Thoreau	The Concord, Massachusetts native was an author, philosopher, and naturalist. He is best known for his writings about independence, spiritual discovery, and self-reliance described in his 1849 essay "Civil Disobedience" and his 1854 book, *Walden*, which was written about a two-year retreat to the woods near Walden Pond. Visit thoreausociety.org or walden.org
1819-1891	Herman Melville	New York city-born Melville is best remembered for his 1851 masterpiece *Moby-Dick*, a novel about a savage whale that destroys a whaling ship, its vengeful captain and crew. Visit melville.org or mobydick.org

1819-1892	Walt Whitman	The West Hills, N.Y.-born Whitman is one of America's greatest poets. He is best known for *Leaves of Grass*, (his Emerson-inspired 1855 poetry collection), and his 1865 poem "O Captain! My Captain!"(about the assassination of President Abraham Lincoln). Visit waltwhitman.org
1830-1886	Emily Dickenson	While leading a solitary life at her family's home in Amherst, Massachusetts, Dickinson, one of the nation's most prolific poets, wrote nearly 1,800 poems. Dickinson's poems were about art, gardens, joy, love, death and grief. Very few of her poems were published during her lifetime. Most of her work was discovered in her bedroom after her death. Visit emilydickinsonmuseum.org
1835-1910	Mark Twain	Born Samuel Clemens in Florida, Missouri, Twain was inspired to write his classic novels *The Adventures of Tom Sawyer*, 1876, and *Adventures of Huckleberry Finn*, 1884, based on his childhood experiences in Hannibal, Missouri, and his job as a Mississippi River steamboat pilot. Twain is known for his witty and satirical prose and the informal dialogue of his characters. He has been called the Father of American Literature. Visit marktwainmuseum.org or marktwainhouse.org

1873-1947	Willa Cather	Born in Virginia's Back Creek Valley in 1873, Cather was 9 years old when her family moved to Red Cloud, Nebraska. She drew inspiration for some of her most famous works— *O, Pioneers!*, *My Antonia*—about life on the American frontier. Visit Willacather.org
1874-1963	Robert Frost	San Francisco-born, the four-time Pulitzer Prize winner wrote much of his poetry about rural New England. Some of his best-known poems, "Birches," "The Road Not Taken" and "Stopping by Woods on a Snowy Evening," were inspired by his life and observations in Massachusetts, New Hampshire and Vermont. Visit frostfriends.org or frostplace.org
1876-1916	Jack London	San Francisco-born London used his experiences as a sailor, gold prospector, and adventurer to write a lot of exciting stories. They included tales about canines in the frozen North and voyages on the high seas in his best-selling novels: *The Call of the Wild*, 1903; *The Sea-Wolf*, 1904; and *White Fang*, 1906. Visit jacklondons.com

1896-1940	F. Scott Fitzgerald	A native of St. Paul, Minnesota, Fitzgerald wrote novels and short stories about optimism, dreams and immoderate actions of the Jazz Age. His works include *This Side of Paradise*, 1920; *The Beautiful and the Damned*, 1922; and *The Great Gatsby*, his 1925 masterpiece. The sales of its first printing were disappointing, but now *The Great Gatsby* is considered among the greatest novels of the 20th century. Visit fscottfitzgeraldsociety.org
1897-1962	William Faulkner	This Mississippi native was a Nobel Prize-winning novelist and short story writer. He described the people, history and settings of his native Mississippi in most of his works, including the literary classics *The Sound and the Fury*, 1929; *Absalom, Absalom!*, 1936; *Go Down, Moses*, 1942; and *The Reivers*, 1962. Visit olemiss.edu/mwp/dir/faulkner_william/
1899-1961	Ernest Hemingway	The Oak Park, Illinois native is considered among the best writers of his generation. He is famous for his action-packed stories about boxing, bullfighting, big-game hunting, fishing, war and human relationships, including the novels *The Sun Also Rises*, 1926; *A Farewell to Arms*, 1929; *For Whom the Bell Tolls*, 1940; and *The Old Man and the Sea*, 1952. Visit timelesshemingway.com

1902-1968	John Steinbeck	A native of Salinas, California, the Nobel Prize- and Pulitzer Prize-winning author awoke the social conscience of the nation with his very interesting stories about California's various ethnic and immigrant groups, migrant workers and sharecroppers. Among his best works are *Of Mice and Men*, 1937; *The Grapes of Wrath*, 1939; and *East of Eden*, 1952. Visit steinbeckhouse.com
1909-1949	Margaret Mitchell	Atlanta, Georgia-born Mitchell wrote *Gone with the Wind*, the best-selling romantic novel about the Civil War in the South. Published in 1936, the novel won the 1937 Pulitzer Prize and since has sold more than 30 million copies. Visit margaretmitchellhouse on Facebook
1919-2010	J.D. Salinger	New York City-born writer, Salinger's 1951 *The Catcher in the Rye* is one of the best-selling American novels of all time, with more than 65 million copies sold. The once shocking story about teenage anxieties, rebellion and sexual desire remains a standard in American literature. Visit deadcaulfields.com
1926-2016	Harper Lee	The Monroeville, Alabama native's only published novel *To Kill a Mockingbird* won her the 1961 Pulitzer Prize for Fiction. This best-seller was about 1930s race relations in the South. Visit harperlee on Facebook

Recommended Reading List for Grades 6-12

Author	Title
Achebe, Chinua	Things Fall Apart
Alcott, Louisa May	Little Women
Anderson, Laurie Halse	Fever 1793
Austen, Jane	Sense and Sensibility
Babbitt, Natalie	Tuck Everlasting
Bradbury, Ray	Fahrenheit 451
Bronte, Charlotte	Jane Eyre
Bronte, Emily	Wuthering Heights
Christie, Agatha	And Then There Were None
Crane, Stephen	The Red Badge of Courage
Creech, Sharon	Walk Two Moons
Dahl, Roald	The BFG
Dickens, Charles	A Tale of Two Cities
Dickens, Charles	Great Expectations
Dickens, Charles	Oliver Twist
Forbes, Esther	Johnny Tremain
Frank, Anne	The Diary of a Young Girl
Hawthorne, Nathaniel	The Scarlett Letter
Hemingway, Ernest	The Old Man and the Sea
Huxley, Aldous	Brave New World
Lee, Harper	To Kill A Mockingbird
L'Engle, Madeleine	A Wrinkle in Time
Levine, Gail Carson	Ella Enchanted
Lowry, Lois	Number the Stars
Lowry, Lois	The Giver
Martel, Yann	Life of Pi
Melville, Herman	Moby Dick
Mitchell, Margaret	Gone With the Wind
Montgomery, L.M.	Anne of Green Gables
O'Dell, Scott	Island of the Blue Dolphins
Paterson, Katherine	Bridge to Terebithia
Rawls, Wilson	Where the Red Fern Grows
Ryan, Pam Munoz	Esperanza Rising
Salinger, J.D.	The Catcher in the Rye
Shakespeare, William	Romeo and Juliet
Steinbeck, John	Of Mice and Men
Steinbeck, John	The Grapes of Wrath
Taylor, Mildred	Roll of Thunder, Hear My Cry
Zusak, Markus	The Book Thief

Appendix G

Presidents of the United States

1. George Washington
   Served: 1789-1797
   Party: None
   Born: February 22, 1732
   Died: December 14, 1799

2. John Adams
   Served: 1797-1801
   Party: Federalist
   Born: October 30, 1735
   Died: July 4, 1826

3. Thomas Jefferson
   Served: 1801-1809
   Party: Democratic-Republican
   Born: April 13, 1743
   Died: July 4, 1826

4. James Madison
   Served: 1809-1817
   Party: Democratic-Republican
   Born: March 16, 1751
   Died: June 28, 1836

5. James Monroe
   Served: 1817-1825
   Party: Democratic-Republican
   Born: April 28, 1758
   Died: July 4, 1831

6. John Quincy Adams
   Served: 1825-1829
   Party: Republican
   Born: July 11, 1767
   Died: February 23, 1848

7. Andrew Jackson
   Served: 1829-1837
   Party: Democrat
   Born: March 15, 1767
   Died: June 8, 1845

8. Martin Van Buren
   Served: 1837-1841
   Party: Party: Democrat
   Born: December 5, 1782
   Died: July 24, 1862

9. William H. Harrison
   Served: 1841
   Party: Whig
   Born: February 9, 1773
   Died: April 4, 1841

10. John Tyler
    Served: 1841-1845
    Party: Whig
    Born: March 29, 1790
    Died: January 18, 1862

11.   James K. Polk
      Served: 1845-1849
      Party: Democrat
      Born: November 2, 1795
      Died: June 15, 1849

12.   Zachary Taylor
      Served: 1849-1850
      Party: Whig
      Born: November 24, 1784
      Died: July 9, 1850

13.   Millard Fillmore
      Served: 1850-1853
      Party: Whig
      Born: January 7, 1800
      Died: March 8, 1874

14.   Franklin Pierce
      Served: 1853-1857
      Party: Democrat
      Born: November 23, 1804
      Died: October 8, 1869

15.   James Buchanan
      Served: 1857-1861
      Party: Democrat
      Born: April 23, 1791
      Died: June 1, 1868

16.   Abraham Lincoln
      Served: 1861-1865
      Party: Republican
      Born: February 12, 1809
      Died: April 15, 1865

17.   Andrew Johnson
      Served: 1865-1869
      Party: Democrat
      Born: December 29, 1808
      Died: July 31, 1875

18.   Ulysses S. Grant
      Served: 1869-1877
      Party: Republican
      Born: April 27, 1822
      Died: July 23, 1885

19.   Rutherford B. Hayes
      Served: 1877-1881
      Party: Republican
      Born: October 4, 1822
      Died: January 17, 1893

20.   James A. Garfield
      Served: 1881
      Party: Republican
      Born: November 19, 1831
      Died: September 19, 1881

21.   Chester A. Arthur
      Served: 1881-1885
      Party: Republican
      Born: October 5, 1829
      Died: November 18, 1886

22.   Grover Cleveland
      Served: 1885-1889
      Party: Democrat
      Born: March 18, 1837
      Died: June 24, 1908

23. Benjamin Harrison
    Served: 1889-1893
    Party: Republican
    Born: August 20, 1833
    Died: March 13, 1901

24. Grover Cleveland
    Served: 1893-1897
    Party: Democrat
    Born: March 18, 1837
    Died: June 24, 1908

25. William McKinley
    Served: 1897-1901
    Party: Republican
    Born: January 29, 1843
    Died: September 14, 1901

26. Theodore Roosevelt
    Served: 1901-1909
    Party: Republican
    Born: October 27, 1858
    Died: January 6, 1919

27. William H. Taft
    Served: 1909-1913
    Party: Republican
    Born: September 15, 1857
    Died: March 8, 1930

28. Woodrow Wilson
    Served: 1913-1921
    Party: Democrat
    Born: December 29, 1856
    Died: February 3, 1924

29. Warren G. Harding
    Served: 1921-1923
    Party: Republican
    Born: November 2, 1865
    Died: August 2, 1923

30. Calvin Coolidge
    Served: 1923-1929
    Party: Republican
    Born: July 4, 1872
    Died: January 5, 1933

31. Herbert C. Hoover
    Served: 1929-1933
    Party: Republican
    Born: August 10, 1874
    Died: October 20, 1964

32. Franklin D. Roosevelt
    Served: 1933-1945
    Party: Democrat
    Born: January 30, 1882
    Died: April 12, 1945

33. Harry S. Truman
    Served: 1945-1953
    Party: Democrat
    Born: May 8, 1884
    Died: December 26, 1972

34. Dwight D. Eisenhower
    Served: 1953-1961
    Party: Republican
    Born: October 14, 1890
    Died: March 28, 1969

35. John F. Kennedy
    Served: 1961-1963
    Party: Democrat
    Born: May 29, 1917
    Died: November 22, 1963

36. Lyndon B. Johnson
    Served: 1963-1969
    Party: Democrat
    Born: August 27, 1908
    Died: January 22, 1973

37.   Richard M. Nixon
       Served: 1969-1974
       Party: Republican
       Born: January 9, 1913
       Died: April 22, 1994

38.   Gerald R. Ford
       Served: 1974-1977
       Party: Republican
       Born: July 14, 1913
       Died: December 26, 2006

39.   James E. Carter, Jr.
       Served: 1977-1981
       Party: Democrat
       Born: October 1, 1924

40.   Ronald W. Reagan
       Served: 1981-1989
       Party: Republican
       Born: February 6, 1911
       Died: June 5, 2004

41.   George H.W. Bush
       Served: 1989-1993
       Party: Republican
       Born: June 12, 1924

42.   William J. Clinton
       Served: 1993-2001
       Party: Democrat
       Born: August 19, 1946

43.   George W. Bush
       Served: 2001-2009
       Party: Republican
       Born: July 6, 1946

44.   Barack H. Obama
       Served: 2009 -
       Party: Democrat
       Born: August 4, 1961

Appendix H

Answer Key to the Study Questions

NOTE: Asterisk * means possible state test question.

Coming to America

<u>Paul Revere</u> warned colonists that the British soldiers were coming.

The <u>Puritans</u> started the Massachusetts Bay Colony.

<u>Jamestown</u> was the first important English settlement in America, and was founded in 1607.

The Pilgrims sailed to America from England in the ship, the <u>Mayflower</u>.

<u>Benjamin Franklin</u> was a leader of the movement to break away from English control. He was famous for many other things, such as being an inventor and publisher.

The <u>Boston Tea Party</u> was a group of Boston colonists who dressed as Mohawk Indians and dumped tea into Boston Harbor. This was to protest the high taxes the King of England made them pay on the tea.

<u>Thomas Paine</u> was the author of *Common Sense*, and he wanted Americans to be free from England and the King.

The <u>Pilgrims</u> left England to avoid religious persecution.

<u>Slavery</u> is when people are owned by other people.

1. The European colonists came to America to claim land and hoped to become wealthy or to escape religious persecution.

2. Native Americans (Indians) lived in America before the Europeans arrived.

3. The Atlantic Ocean is on the East Coast of the United States.

4. People from Africa were taken to America and sold as slaves.

*5. One answer: The Jamestown colonists of Virginia wanted to create their own laws and govern themselves. The Puritan colonists of Massachusetts believed God chose them to govern everyone.
Another answer: The Jamestown colonists came to America to make their fortune and the Puritans came to escape religious persecution in England.

Fight For Self Government

George Washington was the Commander-in-Chief of the Continental (American) Army. He became the first President of the United States of America.

Yankee Doodle was originally an offensive name meaning foolish New Englander. The song eventually became a proud symbol of the courageous, determined and independent American spirit.

A Delegate was a representative of the original American colonies.

British Army soldiers were referred to as "Redcoats" because of the red uniform coats they wore.

Small, local, military units made up of local citizens are called militia.

Hessians were German soldiers who worked for the British.

Benedict Arnold was an American General who committed treason. He agreed to give the fort at West Point, NY to the British in exchange for money.

Marquis de Lafayette was a young, French nobleman who wanted to become an officer in the American Revolutionary army.

The Second Continental Congress was the name of the gathering where delegates from the 13 original colonies began meeting in Philadelphia on May 10, 1775.

1.   Answer can include any three of the following: New Hampshire, Connecticut, Massachusetts, Rhode Island, New York, Pennsylvania, New Jersey, Delaware, Maryland, Virginia, North Carolina, South Carolina, Georgia.

2.   Thomas Jefferson wrote the Declaration of Independence. It was adopted on July 4, 1776.

3.   Answer can include any two of the following: Life, Liberty, Pursuit of Happiness.

4.   The 13 stripes represent the 13 original colonies that became the first states of the United States of America.

Becoming the United States

Additions to the Constitution are called Amendments.

The Federalist Papers were news articles supporting the constitution written by Alexander Hamilton, James Madison and John Jay.

The Bill of Rights are the first ten Amendments to the Constitution.

Checks and Balances is the system created by the Constitution to keep any single branch of government from becoming too powerful.

The Articles of Confederation were created to give states the right to rule themselves and all decisions had to be supported unanimously.

Veto is the power given to the U.S. president to say no to a bill passed by Congress.

1.　　It was hard to get all 13 states to agree completely on every decision. Britain would not sign separate trade agreements with each of the 13 states.

2.　　It was written in 1787. The Constitution creates a strong, central, federal government and gives both state and federal government responsibility for running the country.

3.　　The framers (writers) of the Constitution didn't want any one part of the government to have too much power. By creating the amendment process, no one branch could quickly make legal changes to the U.S. Law.

4.　　"We The People"

5.　　27 Amendments

6.　　Answer can include any of the following: Executive, Legislative or Judicial

7.　　The House of Representatives and the Senate are the two parts of the U.S. Congress.

8.　　Supreme Court

9.　　4 years

10.　　Make U.S. laws, levy taxes, make international agreements, provide for defense of the nation

11.　　The number of Representatives in the House is based on the population of each state.

12.　　The Legislative branch writes laws. They must be passed by the House of Representatives and the Senate.

13.　　Serve on a jury, vote in all elections

14.　　Life, Liberty and the Pursuit of Happiness

15.　　Two of the rights of everyone living in the United States are Freedom of Speech and Freedom of Religion.

16.　　The judicial branch interprets the constitution and reviews the laws made by Congress.

17.　　9

*18.　　The right of privacy means protection against unlawful governmental entry without proper authority.

*19. Civilian control is an important feature of a stable democracy. Military people must follow orders without question, but civilians don't, so the leader should be free from all pressure. Presidents can be removed by Congress if necessary, but generals can't.

First Government

Sacajawea was a female Native American teenager who helped Lewis and Clark on their journey to the Pacific Ocean.

Francis Scott Key wrote a poem called the Star Spangled Banner that later became our national anthem.

A fort is a defensive structure built to protect a region and the people living there.

Meriwether Lewis explored the northwest portion of the U.S. with William Clark.

John Adams was the second President of the United States.

Alexander Hamilton was in President Washington's Cabinet, and he did not believe all people were equal. He wanted a strong federal government with a national bank.

The Louisiana Purchase was a territory bought from France in 1803. The land purchased contained all of present-day Arkansas, Missouri, Iowa, Oklahoma, Kansas, and Nebraska; parts of Minnesota that were west of the Mississippi River; most of North Dakota; most of South Dakota; northeastern New Mexico; northern Texas; the portions of Montana, Wyoming, and Colorado east of the Continental Divide; Louisiana west of the Mississippi River, including the city of New Orleans; and small portions of land that would eventually become part of the Canadian provinces of Alberta and Saskatchewan.

The War of 1812 was the war fought between the U.S. and England over control of the Canadian territory.

The Capitol is the building where Congress meets and passes laws.

1.   The name of the National Anthem is The Star-Spangled Banner.
2.   The capital of the United States is Washington, DC.
3.   The Pacific Ocean is on the west coast of the United States.
4.   Answer can include either of the following: Mississippi, Missouri
5.   Cabinet members advise the President on their areas of the Federal Government.
     Answer can include any two of the following: Secretary of State, Secretary of the Treasury, Secretary of Defense, Attorney General,

Secretary of the Interior, Secretary of Agriculture, Secretary of Commerce, Secretary of Labor, Secretary of Health and Human Services, Secretary of Housing and Urban Development, Secretary of Transportation, Secretary of Energy, Secretary of Education, Secretary of Veterans Affairs, Secretary of Homeland Security

First Expansion of the United States

The <u>Monroe Doctrine</u> was established by President Monroe. It warned the European countries not to interfere with the New World. In return, the U.S. would not interfere with European wars or politics.

<u>Seminole</u> was a Native American Indian tribe located in Florida.

The <u>Oregon Trail</u> was an American pioneer trail which started in Independence, Missouri and went to Boise, Idaho, then through the mountains to the Willamette Valley in Oregon.

<u>Andrew Jackson</u> was elected President of the U.S. in 1828.

A <u>self-made man</u> was a man who succeeded through his own efforts and not because he was born rich or with special advantages.

<u>Impeachment</u> means to officially charge and try a U.S. president for an offense. It does not mean remove from the presidency. Andrew Jackson was the first president to be impeached.

The <u>Santé Fe Trail</u> was an American pioneer trail which started in Independence, Missouri and went to Santé Fe, New Mexico where it connected with the trail down into Mexico.

The <u>Trail of Tears</u> is the name given by the Cherokee Indians from Georgia, Tennessee and the Carolinas, to the last 800 miles travelled by foot to Oklahoma. About one-fourth of the Indians died on the journey.

<u>Prairie Schooners</u> were big covered wagons that American pioneers used to travel west.

<u>General Santa Anna</u> was the Mexican Army General in America's war with Mexico.

1.　　The Louisiana Purchase more than doubled the area of the United States.
2.　　a)　　War: The Mexican-American War added New Mexico, Arizona, California, Nevada, Utah and Colorado to the U.S.
　　　　b)　　Purchase: Florida was bought from Spain. The Louisiana Purchase from France added land west of the Mississippi River and north of the Missouri River west all the way to the

shore of the Pacific Ocean. The U.S. gained 828,000 square miles of territory.

c) Rebellion: The Seminoles in Florida and the Cherokee in Georgia, Tennessee, and the Carolinas rebelled against the Indian Removal Act and they were defeated and sent to Oklahoma.

d) Exchange: The Congress passed the Indian Removal Act which allowed the U.S. government to remove Native Americans from their lands and relocate them to other states.

*3. Manifest Destiny was appealing to the American people in the 1840's because they believed that God wanted Americans to keep moving west until the United States reached the Pacific Ocean.

Reform in the United States

Frederick Douglass was a former slave who became an abolitionist.
Dorothea Dix was a schoolteacher and author. She is remembered most for her work in improving treatment of the mentally ill.
Susan B. Anthony joined with Elizabeth Cady Stanton in founding the National Woman Suffrage Association to fight for the women's right to vote.
Abolitionists were reformers who wanted to end slavery.
Horace Mann improved education in the United States. He believed that all children should learn to read and write.
The Temperance Movement was a group of reformers who wanted people to stop drinking alcohol.
Elizabeth Cady Stanton was an abolitionist known best for being an advocate for women's rights.
The Seneca Falls Convention was held in July 1848, where about 100 men and women met at Seneca Falls, NY to discuss women's rights. They wrote a declaration that all men AND women are created equal.

1. Universal education is the ability of all individuals to have equal opportunity in education, regardless of social class, gender, ethnicity background or physical and mental disabilities.
2. Elizabeth Cady Stanton and Susan B. Anthony founded the National Woman Suffrage Association.
*3. The Homestead Act of 1862 gave 160 acres to each homesteader who lived on the land and farmed it. This opened the floodgates of western settlement.

A Nation Divided

Ulysses. S. Grant was the Commander of the Union Army.

The Gettysburg Address was Lincoln's speech dedicating Gettysburg as a National Cemetery. He talked about the Declaration of Independence, reminding people of the U.S. ideals. The U.S. is not a collection of states, but a unified nation.

The Confederacy was the unified southern states that left the Union (United States).

Secession was the act of a southern state leaving the Union (United States).

Uncle Tom's Cabin was a book written by Harriett Beecher Stowe that inspired Northerners to oppose slavery.

Robert E. Lee was the Commander of the Confederate Army.

Dred Scott was a slave whose owner moved him from the slave state of Missouri to the free state of Wisconsin, then back to Missouri. Dred Scott felt he and his family should continue to be free as they had been in Wisconsin. However, the courts decided against him saying they were property and an owner was free to take his property with him wherever he goes.

Jefferson Davis was the President of the Confederate States of America.

Harriet Tubman was a former slave who was a "conductor" in the Underground Railroad. She was also a spy for the Union Army during the Civil War.

William Tecumseh Sherman led troops into the center of the Confederacy in the spring of 1864. During his "march" from Atlanta, GA to Savannah, GA, his troops formed a line 60 miles wide, destroying everything in their path.

The Emancipation Proclamation as issued by Lincoln, stating that effective January 1, 1863, all the slaves in the Confederacy would be free.

Appomattox Court House was the village in Virginia where Lee surrendered to Grant and this act ended the Civil War.

The Underground Railroad was a secret route by which escaped slaves could use safe houses to travel north to freedom.

1.   Slavery is one problem that led to the Civil War. Another problem was the difference in the economies between the North and the South.

2.   The main effect of the Missouri Compromise was to keep a balance in the number of free vs. slave states. One free state had to be added for each slave state added.

3.   The Civil War was the U.S. war between the North and the South.

4. Answer can include any of the following: He was elected President. He saved the Union (United States of America). He freed the slaves.

5. The Emancipation Proclamation freed the slaves.

*6. John Brown was an abolitionist who believed so strongly in freedom for blacks that he was willing to act violently. In October 1859, he led 18 men, including 5 free African Americans in an attempt to capture weapons at Harpers Ferry, VA. He planned to arm slaves for rebellion. His plan failed, and he was captured and hung.
Harriett Beecher Stowe convinced many Northerners that slavery was wrong, based on her novel *Uncle Tom's Cabin*.
Harriet Tubman was a former slave, and a "conductor" in the Underground Railroad, as well as a spy for the Union Army during the Civil War.

*7. Many answers are possible but must include all items in the question. Below are some ideas to help with your response:

   a) The Constitution was created for all people and the Bill of Rights clearly states what additional rights Americans had. Lincoln always talked about these ideals.

   b) Colonists fought for their independence from the British, set up government of, for, and by the people, with no kings. The Constitution was written by representatives of the people and clearly designed each part of the government and their jobs.

   c) Lincoln insisted that the Civil War was being fought, not over slavery, but to reunite the nation. Some northern border states allowed slavery. He was worried that if he took too strong a stand against slavery, those states would join the Confederacy. Grant's surrender terms to Lee were generous; he was also focused on reuniting the nation.

   d) During the acceptance of the new Constitution, the Federalists party and the anti-Federalist party argued about their vision of the future of the U.S. government system. In the years leading up to the Civil War, a new political party was formed called the Republican Party. It was strongly opposed to slavery. Abraham Lincoln was a member of the Republican Party.

   e) The Civil War increased the Federal Government's power and authority, including getting taxes to pay for the war, and creation of a permanent military. Economic growth increased, at least in the northern states.

Reunification and Growth

Carpetbaggers were Northerners who came to the South carrying bags made from carpets. Some did take advantage of Southerners, but most wanted to help.

The Ku Klux Klan was a secret organization formed to scare blacks, and whites who were friendly to blacks. They wore white hoods and set fires to crosses, as well as black churches, schools and houses.

The 14th Amendment was passed on July 9, 1868. It says that all persons born in the U.S. are citizens of the U.S. No state may deprive any person of life, liberty or property without due process of law, giving every person a chance to defend his rights in court.

White Southerners who did not like the new state governments called the people who supported the new governments, scalawags.

To keep blacks from voting, some southern governments implemented a poll tax requiring a payment to vote. Most blacks could not afford the tax, and so they could not vote.

The 15th Amendment was passed by Congress on February 26, 1869. It forbids state governments from limiting or denying anyone's rights because of race, color, or the fact that they were once a slave.

John Wilkes Booth was a man who believed in slavery and had supported the Confederacy. He shot Abraham Lincoln in the head and killed him at Ford's Theater in Washington, DC on April 14, 1865. He was captured and killed by U.S. soldiers.

The Freedmen's Bureau was created to help African Americans. It did not provide the freed slaves 40 acres and a mule they believed they would receive, but it did build schools and colleges for blacks across the South.

The Reconstruction lasted from 1865-1877. It was the process of bringing the 11 former Confederate states back into the Union (United States).

1.   Economic growth, industry and farming increased in the North and Midwest, but destroyed most of the industry and farming in the South. It took the South years to recover. For the former slaves, freedom was a mixed blessing. They were left with no property, no jobs, no homes, and were the target of white Southerner's anger over what they had lost. It was hard to survive.

Shortly before the end of the war, the Freedmen's Bureau was created to give small plots of land to blacks. Congress did give the Freedmen's Bureau control of millions of acres of land for freed slaves, but then President Johnson gave it back to its' former white owners.

2.   President Johnson was impeached for repeatedly trying to block reconstruction. No other president had ever been impeached before.

*3.   President Bill Clinton was impeached on two charges: perjury and obstruction of justice.

*4.   Black codes were laws that denied blacks their basic rights, including the right to vote. They also limited blacks' ability to own property and work in certain trades and businesses.

Second Expansion of the United States

The Gold Rush was the name given to movement of people going west to search for gold. John Sutter saw flakes of yellow metal in the water that ran through his mill. News of this discovery spread quickly and thousands of people headed to California hoping to get rich.

The Homestead Act was passed in 1862. It gave 160 acres of land to every head of household, including women and former slaves, if they worked the land for five years.

The Sioux were one of the main eastern Plain tribes.

Thomas Edison invented/patented more than 1000 devices and processes including the phonograph and the first light bulb.

The Pony Express was a form of mail delivery. Riders on horseback carrying the mail, would ride as fast as they could, changing horses every ten miles. This was repeated all the way from Missouri to San Francisco, California.

In 1863, the Central Pacific Railroad started laying track in California and headed east.

In 1864, the Union Pacific Railroad started from Nebraska and headed west. The Central Pacific and Union Pacific Railroads linked their tracks at Promontory Point, Utah in 1869.

*1.   The immigrant population expanded creating pressure in the cities for jobs and homes. People from many different cultures moved out of the cities and westward looking for a better life.

2.   The transcontinental railroad moved people and goods from coast to coast and helped expand the national economy.

3.   Three major Native American tribes in the U.S. can include any of the following: Cherokee, Seminole, Delaware, Susquehanna, Mohican, Massachusett, Algonquin, Apache, Navajo, Chinook, Nez Perce, Sioux, Dakota and Lakota.

*4.   As a result of treaties and wars, the United States gained more land.

a)   The division and then reunification of Northern and Southern states and the addition of the new states expanded the area of the U.S.

b)   In 1877, most people lived east of Kansas. West of Kansas were mainly Native Americans who were not considered American citizens. The westward movement of the immigrants forced the Native Americans into smaller areas and also less desirable locations.

c)   People and goods could be moved across the country with the completion of the transcontinental railroad. The telegraph allowed cross country communication in a timely manner.

The Wild West

The Apache is a Native American tribe of the Southwest who were known as fierce fighters.

Sitting Bull was a Native American Tribal Leader.

A patent is a special right awarded to an inventor who proves that his invention is both new and useful.

Alexander Graham Bell invented the telegraph which transmitted sound using Morse code. He also invented the telephone.

Pueblo was the name the Spanish called the Native American tribes of the Southwest.

Little Big Horn was a stream where General George Armstrong Custer attacked Native Americans including Sitting Bull and Crazy Horse. The battle is referred to as "Custer's Last Stand" as he died here.

George Washington Carver was born a slave and became an important African American scientist and inventor. He earned an advanced college degree and discovered hundreds of uses for the peanut.

Nez Perce was the name the French traders called the Tsutpoli tribe. The name means pierced nose because some of the tribe wore rings in their noses.

White Americans thought they were helping Native Americans by teaching them to be more like white Americans. This process was called assimilation.

1.   New Mexico, Louisiana and Oregon were all U.S. territories.

2.   The passing of the Homestead Act provided the motivation for many people to move west. The government was also successful in taking more of the Native Americans' land. The Native Americans were forced to leave their homes and live on reservations.

*3. While the Dawes Act gave each Native American household 160 acres, most Native Americans were poor and had to sell the land. This allowed white Americans to gain more of the reservation land.

*4. Their children were being taught to reject their Native ways and customs.

*5. The Statue of Liberty is located in New York Harbor. It symbolizes freedom.

*6. North American Indian culture: They hunted on foot, believed no single person owned land and that it belonged to the tribe, and considered the Black Hills to be sacred ground.
White Settlers of the Great Plains: They hunted on horseback, believed individuals owned land, and considered the Black Hills to be valuable land after gold was discovered there in 1874.

Industrialization in the United States

Industry owners were called Capitalists.

John D. Rockefeller was the owner of Standard Oil Co. and he took over oil processing plants which are called refineries.

Populism is defined as a political doctrine that appeals to the interests of the general population, especially contrasting those interests with the interests of the elite.

A Monopoly is an exclusive control over an industry or economic market. Huge monopolies came to be called trusts.

Labor Unions were groups of workers who banded together to demand better pay and better working conditions from management and the owners.

Andrew Carnegie owned many steel factories and became rich because the expanding railroad needed steel.

Workers would "strike" (stop working), if their demands for more pay or better working conditions were not met.

J.P. Morgan gained a monopoly over the U.S. system of banks. He became extremely wealthy.

1. Workers formed Unions to demand better pay and working conditions.

2. With no iron ore and coal, there would be no raw materials to make steel, which was needed for the expanding railroads. The railroads helped move raw materials to the factories.

*3.   Many answers are possible but below are some points to help you
        with your answer:
   a)   Raw materials could be easily transported by rail or shipped
          on rivers throughout the country.
   b)   People from around the world saw the United States as a
          land of opportunity, so they came to the U.S. to find work. As
          the cities became crowded, they moved west in search
          of work.
   c)   Small groups of industrial leaders dominated the United
          States' most important industries. The owners became rich.
          The workers did not.
   d)   Machinery now did many jobs previously done by humans.

Social Change

Settlement House was the name given to community centers that provided
food, shelter and services to the poor.
Puerto Rico is a U.S. territory that had belonged to Spain until 1898.
Booker T. Washington believed that education was necessary for African
Americans to improve their lives.
Muckrakers were journalists who wrote about the "ugly" side of life in the
United States, such as corruption in business practices and what life was
like for the poor in America.
Philanthropists are people who give part of their wealth helping others who
are less fortunate. Famous philanthropists were mainly rich capitalists like
Andrew Carnegie.
Yellow Journalism was the name given to newspaper reporting that
stretched the truth or made up lies in order to sell more newspapers.
NAACP stands for National Association for the Advancement of Colored
People, which was formed by W.E.B. Du Bois and other reformers.
Jane Addams was neither poor or from a big city, but she was determined
to help the less fortunate. She opposed prejudice against immigrants.
The USS Maine was the battleship sent by the U.S. Navy to Cuba in 1898,
not to attack, but to help Americans that were caught in the middle of the
war between Spain and Cubans (who wanted their independence from
Spain). On February 15, 1898, an explosion on the USS Maine killed 260
Americans and the ship sank. Studies today say the explosion may have
been an accident, but in 1898, yellow journalists blamed Spain.

1. The Panama Canal allowed for easier shipping between the Atlantic and Pacific Oceans.

2. Someone could volunteer their time at, and donate supplies to settlement houses.

3. Easier movement of goods and of people across the country, made railroads and their owners, successful and rich. The easier movement of raw materials to the factories made it easier to make goods.

4. Settlements houses provided food, shelter and services to improve the lives of the poor. NAACP fought for equality for African Americans. Jane Addams opened a settlement house called Hull House in Chicago, IL. W.E.B. Du Bois said that African Americans should insist loudly upon the equal rights promised to them by the 14th Amendment. He formed the Niagara movement and started the NAACP.

*5. Many answers are possible but below are some points to help you with your answer:

    a)   Declaration of Independence – Many Americans believed that establishing an empire (American territories all over the world), violated the principles of the Declaration of Independence, because it didn't allow the territories to govern themselves. While the Declaration of Independence states that all men are created equal, in the late 1800's, African Americans were still denied equal opportunity to better themselves.

    b)   The U.S. Constitution created a strong, central government to keep government of, by and for the people. The Federal government eventually put controls on big business so that wealth would not be available to only a few people.

    c)   Bill of Rights – The Bill of Rights was made to protect our rights and freedoms. In the U.S., we continue to have freedom of speech, religion, the press, as well as the right to protect ourselves, privacy and trial by jury.

    d)   The Gettysburg Address – Reminded the American people of the founding ideals and help the divided country to reunite after the Civil War.

    e)   The 13th Amendment made slavery illegal in the U.S., and people more equal. The 14th Amendment says that all persons born or naturalized in the U.S. are U.S. citizens. States cannot deny citizens life, liberty, or property without due process of law or deny any citizen equal protection of the laws. The 15th Amendment

granted African American men the right to vote by
declaring that the right of citizens of the U.S. to vote
shall not be denied or abridged by the U.S. or any state,
because of race, color, or previous condition of servitude.
This was not fully realized for almost a century due to
the use of poll taxes and literacy tests. Before the
Voting Rights Act of 1965, most African Americans in
the South were not registered to vote. The 15th Amendment
reinforced the idea of equality, but was very difficult to get
local states to support.

Moving Into the World

Suffrage is the word for the right to vote.

The League of Nations was meant to be an assembly where nations could
meet and settle conflicts peacefully.

Amelia Earhart became the first woman to fly solo from New York to Paris
in 1932. In 1937, she tried to fly around the world, however, she and her
airplane disappeared in the South Pacific.

Creationism is the belief that the world was created by the Christian God
in 7 days, as told in the Bible.

Charlie Chaplin was an early 20th century actor. He performed mostly in
silent comedies.

Flappers was a term for fun loving, carefree young women who visited
speakeasies. Flappers also smoked and wore dresses that showed their legs.

Langston Hughes was a poet who said that African American artists and
writers should please themselves with their work, not white Americans.

Evolution is the theory that humans evolved from animals such as apes.

Charles Lindbergh was a pilot and he became the first person to fly solo
from New York to Paris in 1927.

Communism was a belief developed by Karl Marx. He thought it was wrong
that just a few were rich and powerful. He wanted to overthrow the rich,
ruling class, so that all could be equal. In reality, communists were a small
minority who kept the power for themselves.

The Harlem Renaissance was a period in American history from 1918 to
1937 that included a marked rise in the number of African American artists,
writers and scholars. Many of these people lived in Harlem, NY.

The 18th Amendment prohibited the making and selling of beer, wine and
alcohol.

1. The U.S. was involved in many wars and conflicts during the 1900's. They included World War I (originally called the Great War), World War II, the Korean War, the Viet Nam War, the Bay of Pigs Invasion, and the U.S. invasion of Panama.

2. At the beginning of World War I, Germany and England were blockading each other's harbors. The United States remained neutral as long as possible as they were horrified by the brutality of the war. The United States eventually entered the war after a German U-Boat (submarine) sank a passenger ship with Americans on board. Germany also asked Mexico to help them in the war. In exchange, Germany would help Mexico gain back some territory it had lost in the Mexican American War. This offer, plus the U-Boat actions convinced the U.S. to enter the war.

3. Woodrow Wilson was U.S. President during World War I.

4. Weapons such as tanks, airplanes, submarines, poison gas and machine guns made World War I more deadly than previous wars. Machine guns could fire 400 bullets a minute.

5. During Prohibition, Americans were not allowed to drink beer, wine and alcohol. Many drank in secret though, at illegal bars called speakeasies. This created a demand for these items which lead to an increase in illegal activities and the growth of an illegal industry. It helped develop organized crime.

*6. Most American homes had electricity, allowing people to enjoy new devices such as the radio, vacuum cleaner, washing machines, stoves and refrigerators. Mass production of automobiles made auto ownership available to the average person, allowing freedom of movement.

*7. American ties with the Allies (France, England) were stronger than its ties with the Central Powers because France had helped the U.S. in the Revolutionary War. In addition, many of the U.S. ideals were based on English ideals.

The Depression Years

The <u>Hoover Dam</u> was built to provide electricity and flood control for the Colorado River Basin.

A <u>stock</u> is a share in a company, as if you own a small piece of the company. Shares can be bought and sold.

The <u>New Deal</u> was President Franklin Delano Roosevelt's plan to get the United States out of the Depression. It included the 3 Rs – Relief, Recovery and Reform.

The <u>Great Depression</u> was a period in American history in the 1930's. Millions of Americans lost their jobs, homes and struggled to feed their families.

<u>Deficit Spending</u> means spending more money than you receive.

The <u>Civilian Conservation Corps</u> was a New Deal program that provided jobs for men ages 18-25. They would work on projects to protect the environment.

The <u>Indian Reorganization Act</u> was a government law that stopped Indian land allotments and provided money to buy land for Native Americans.

1. Texas, Oklahoma, Kansas, Nebraska, Colorado and the Dakotas were included in the Dust Bowl region.

2. The price of stocks fell drastically so the companies had no money to keep. It led to the Great Depression. People lost their jobs, and couldn't afford to pay for their houses, cars, etc. Factories closed.

3. Five New Deal agencies that are still around today: FDIC (Federal Deposit Insurance Corporation), SEC (Securities and Exchange Commission), TVA (Tennessee Valley Authority), FHA (Federal Housing Administration), and Social Security Administration and the National Labor Relations Board (created by the Wagner Act).

*4. Many answers are possible but below are some points to help you with your answer:

a) The Tennessee Valley Authority taught farmers in the Tennessee Valley region better ways to grow crops. They reduced the loose soil in the Dust Bowl Region. The Civilian Conservation Corps hired unemployed young men and they fought forest fires and planted trees to fight against the Dust Bowl. Dams were built to control flooding and harness the river power for electricity. Unemployment – President Roosevelt's Works Progress Administration put men to work on building projects across the United States. The Wagner Act of 1935 protected worker's rights. Government subsidies helped farmers get a fair price for their crops. Social Security programs were introduced to provide for the elderly and poor.

b) The Wagner Act of 1935 introduced labor policies that protected the rights of workers. The Social Security program was developed to provide for the unemployed, the sick and the elderly. You pay into the fund while you are able to work. If you are old, sick or lose your job, you receive money from these funds. Banking and financial regulations created the Federal Deposit Insurance Corporation. Money you put in the bank, was now guaranteed to be there when you needed it. Government job programs focused on protecting and improving the environment. Crop subsidies helped farmers received a fair price for their crops.

*5.   Yes. You need people to have or be making money so they can spend it on products, thus creating jobs for others.

The War Years

Rosie the Riveter was a fictional character representing the millions of women who joined the labor force working in factories building heavy machinery during World War II.

The Blitzkrieg or "Lightning War" was the name given to powerful attacks on other countries by Hitler's army.

Dwight Eisenhower was an American General in World War II who led the big invasion of France to fight the Germans. He was eventually elected President after the war.

Winston Churchill was the British Prime Minister during World War II in the 1940's.

In February 1945, Allied leaders Churchill, Roosevelt and Stalin, met in Yalta in the Soviet Union to discuss what would happen after the war.

Nazi was the term used for someone belonging to Germany's National Socialist Party. The most well-known Nazi, Chancellor Hitler, declared himself dictator of Germany. Nazis believed they were superior to other ethnic groups and they especially hated the Jews.

The Holocaust was the name given to the mass murder of Jews in concentration camps, mostly in gas chambers, by the German army.

Genocide is the deliberate killing of large groups of people, usually a particular ethnic group or nation.

The Axis Powers were Japan, Germany and Italy during World War II.

Fascism was a belief system like the Nazi's in Germany. It was predominate in Italy and led by Benito Mussolini, the dictator in Italy.

Starting in 1942, the United States government interred Japanese Americans in camps until 1944, because the government believed that the Japanese Americans might be spies for Japan.

The <u>Atomic Bomb</u> was a bomb made by the splitting of atoms which releases an inconceivable amount of energy. President Truman knew that if the war continued, thousands more lives would be lost. To get Japan to surrender, he ordered atomic bombs to be dropped on Hiroshima, Japan on August 6, 1945 and Nagasaki, Japan on August 9, 1945.

The <u>Battle of Midway</u> was the name of a very important battle in WWII that was a turning point in the Pacific war. In June 1942, Japanese planes attacked a group of Pacific Islands occupied by the United States. The United States fought the battle in the air and stopped the Japanese movement across the Pacific Ocean.

1. After the Japanese attacked the United States military at Pearl Harbor, Hawaii on December 7, 1941, the United States declared war on Japan on December 8, 1941.

2. The significance of the Battle of Stalingrad was that Germany attacked the Soviet Union expecting to control the natural resources in that area. Germany was ultimately defeated by the region's harsh winters.

3. The automobile factories were redesigned to manufacture weapons, tanks, and airplanes. The United States also coordinated the research of scientists who were working on the possibility of an atomic bomb. This research was called The Manhattan Project.

4. President Truman decided to use the atomic bomb to hasten the surrender of the Japanese.

*5. Yes or no and explain your reasoning.

*6. Many answers are possible but below are some points to help you with your answer:

a) Economic – the war put people to work, Military – the A bomb brought about "Cold War," Social resources – It brought women into the military but in administrative jobs. World War II helped the U.S. economy to grow because of the demand for war materials and it expanded the role of women into more non-traditional jobs.

b) Role of women – Women worked in the factories while the men were away fighting the war, Role of minorities – Tuskegee Airmen – This was the popular name of a group of African American military pilots who fought in World War II.

c) The internment of Japanese Americans and other of Asian background happened because of mistrust.

Becoming a World Example

<u>The Iron Curtain</u> was the imaginary barrier that separated eastern communist governments from western democratic governments.

<u>The Marshall Plan</u> was created in 1948. The United States spent billions of dollars to rebuild the western European economy.

<u>The H-Bomb</u> was more powerful than the Atomic Bomb. The H-Bomb worked by slamming atoms together, rather than splitting them apart.

In the early 1950's, the United States fought communism in <u>Korea</u> when North Korea invaded South Korea. A United Nations army pushed North Korea all the way back to the Chinese border, but China joined in and fought back. The Koreas remain divided today.

<u>NATO</u> (North Atlantic Treaty Organization) was an alliance formed In 1949 between 12 nations including Belgium, Denmark, France, Great Britain, Iceland, Italy, Luxembourg, The Netherlands, Norway, Portugal, the United States and Canada. They promised each other military support if the other members were attacked. This organization has expanded today to include many more European nations.

The <u>United Nations</u> is a world organization of countries where complaints and issues can be discussed by all members. A council of 5 countries is used to vote on the more complex issues that affect all the nations. It replaced the League of Nations in 1945.

The <u>Cold War</u> was a tense "war" between the U.S.S.R. and the U.S. It was not fought with bullets and bombs but with threats. Both countries increased military forces during this period from 1946-1991.

The <u>Suburbs</u> are middle class communities surrounding large cities.

In 1947, President Truman promised, that the U.S. would help any country to resist any threat of communism. This was called the <u>Truman Doctrine</u>.

<u>McCarthyism</u> was named after Senator Joe McCarthy, who accused 205 people of being communists. His negative tactics made him famous. Eventually Americans saw him as a bully and a liar.

<u>G.I.</u> is slang for Government Issue servicemen.

1.   U.S.S.R. supported North Korea's invasion of South Korea.

2.   During the Cold War, the main concern of the U.S. was preventing the spread of communism.

3.   Agree. Both sides were increasing their nuclear power at an alarming rate which would be devastating if it was used.

*4.   Many answers are possible but below are some points to help you with your answer:

a)   Differences in political beliefs and values, and the economic and governmental institutions:

U.S.	U.S.S.R.
1) Democratic-Citizens elect government officials	1) Totalitarian –Government controls every part of its citizens' economic, political, and social lives
2) Rights guaranteed by Constitution	2) Denied freedom of speech, press and religion
3) Capitalist – citizens control their own economic actions	3) Communist government controls all property and economic activity

b)   Actions by the U.S. and U.S.S.R. in the last years of World War II and after. Use of Atomic Bomb – The U.S. had used it already, the U.S.S.R. developed it a few years after, to use on the U.S. if necessary. The U.S. spent billions of dollars to rebuild western Europe's economy which helped those countries to remain democratic and helped the U.S. economy as well. The Truman Doctrine promised to help any country threatened by communism, which upset the U.S.S.R. NATO – started with 12 countries promising each other military support if attacked, further upsetting the U.S.S.R.

Civil Rights in Post WWI America

NASA stands for the National Aeronautics and Space Administration.
Sputnik was the first man-made satellite, launched in 1957 by U.S.S.R.
In the early 1960s, the U.S. and U.S.S.R. argued over Germany's capital city Berlin. The U.S.S.R. leader Nikita Krushchev wanted the British, French, and American citizens to leave. President Kennedy refused so Krushchev built the Berlin Wall, separating East Berlin from West Berlin.
Martin Luther King, Jr. was a young black minister who led the Montgomery boycott. He was assassinated in 1968.
Rosa Parks refused to give up her bus seat to a white man. She was arrested for breaking a Jim Crow law.

<u>Nation of Islam</u> is sometimes called Black Muslims; they claim to be followers of Islam, but in their version, blacks are superior to whites. This version opposed the actual teachings of Islam which says all races are equal.
The <u>Great Society</u> was an anti-poverty plan created by President Lyndon Johnson.
<u>Brown vs. the Board of Education</u> was a Supreme Court case regarding Linda Brown, a black child who was not allowed to attend the white school which was closer to her home. The court's decision stated that segregation violated the rights of African-American students.
<u>Fidel Castro</u> created the communist government in Cuba in 1959. He had strong ties to the U.S.S.R.
The <u>Peace Corps</u> is a government program, introduced by President Kennedy. Peace Corp members work in poor countries helping build roads, buildings, teaching new farming methods, and developing health programs.
<u>Malcolm X</u> became a follower of Islam while in prison. He was a powerful speaker regarding the rights of African Americans. He was assassinated in 1965.

1.   Since Martin Luther King, Jr. was a Christian, he followed Christ's teaching which says to love everyone, even those who want to harm you. He was also influenced by the great non-violent Indian leader, Mahatma Gandhi, and American writer, Henry David Thoreau.
2.   Yes. Martin Luther King, Jr. wanted the people to quietly but firmly disobey unjust laws. He hoped that these actions would save lives but also change the rules.
3.   The Civil Rights Movement tried to end racial discrimination.
*4.   Martin Luther King, Jr. supported passive resistance; Malcolm X wanted African Americans to fight for their rights. The methods of Martin Luther King, Jr. were more effective because positive changes were brought about using his methods.
5.   As a result of the Cuban missile crisis in 1963, Americans and Russians began to work on an agreement that controlled nuclear weapons so that nations would not come so close to war.
6.   Yes. He said, "Ask not what your country can do for you, but what you can do for your country." He believed that a nation is only as strong as its citizens.
*7.   Many answers are possible but below are some points to help you with your answer:

a)   President Truman integrated the Armed Forces (military) in 1948. Blacks and whites first served together in the Korean War.

b)   Brown vs. Board of Education – In 1954, Thurgood Marshall argued Brown vs. Board of Education representing Linda Brown, the 3rd grader not allowed to attend the white school which was closer to her home. The Supreme Court agreed that segregated schools violated the rights of African American students. The Civil Rights Act (1957) protected voting rights. The Civil Rights Act (1964) made it illegal to discriminate based on race, religion and ethnicity. The Voting Rights Act (1965) ended the tricks such as poll taxes which kept many blacks from voting.

c)   The Montgomery Bus Boycott (1955-1956) – African Americans refused to ride buses until blacks and whites were treated equally. The bus companies were losing money because most of the riders were black. The Supreme Court ruled that segregated buses were unconstitutional. The March on Washington (1963) – Held in Washington, DC on August 28, 1963. Over 200,000 people marched (25% were white), to show support for the Civil Rights Act of 1963. National Association for the Advancement of Colored People (NAACP) decided in 1950, that public schools should not be segregated. Nation of Islam – sometimes called Black Muslims, however, their teachings did not follow the actual teachings of Islam. These events helped the American society to develop less discriminatory practices in all areas, for example: business, government, and education.

A Time of Great Changes

In 1965, there was a group of communist guerillas called the Viet Cong who tried to overthrow the South Vietnamese government.

The Bicentennial is the 200th birthday of a country; for the U.S., it was July 4, 1976.

In 1968, according to President Johnson, the policy of self-determination gave Native Americans a choice to remain in their homelands, without surrendering dignity, OR to move to cities and towns across America equipped with skills to live in equality and dignity.

Feminism is a belief in equal rights and opportunities for women.

<u>Watergate</u> was a political scandal where five men broke into the Democratic Party Office in the Watergate Hotel, looking for embarrassing information about the candidates.

<u>Cesar Chavez</u> was a Mexican American, who led the movement to improve the lives of migrant workers.

<u>Betty Friedan</u> is the author of "The Feminine Mystique" published in 1963. She said that the housewife "trap" made American women unhappy.

<u>NOW</u> was the National Organization for Women. It was created in 1966.

<u>Guerillas</u> are fighters who are not part of the regular army.

<u>Neil Armstrong</u> was the first man to set foot on the moon on July 20, 1969.

The <u>draft</u> was a government system established to fill vacancies in the U.S. military. It required all young men, at age 18, to serve in the U.S. military for 2-4 years. The draft was stopped in 1973. Now U.S. military service is voluntary.

*1. The hippies often did not complete their education so they were unable to earn enough money to pay for food and shelter for themselves and their families.

2. A president can misuse power by stopping investigations into a crime, similar to what President Nixon did on Watergate.

*3. Rule of Law – Laws should govern a nation. Example: The smooth transition from Nixon's resignation to President Ford's inauguration. Violence was not necessary for a change in government or its leader.

*4. The Women's Rights movement encouraged women to seek non-traditional roles. Women didn't have to be only teachers and nurses, but they could be doctors, lawyers, or anything they chose. They could still be homemakers if they wished, but they had a choice. The ERA never passed. People felt that the Civil Rights Act of 1964 had already established equality for women.

The Changing World

<u>NAFTA</u> is the North American Free Trade Agreement. It created Free Trade with Canada and Mexico.

<u>Desert Storm</u> was a U.S. military operation where the U.S. military was sent to protect Kuwait after Iran invaded the country in an attempt to take over Kuwait's oil wells.

A <u>millennium</u> is 1000 years.

Middle Eastern terrorists hijacked airplanes and flew them into the <u>World Trade Center</u> in New York City.

The <u>Department of Homeland Security</u> is the government department created in response to the September 11, 2001 attacks. It manages security at airports, train stations and seaports as well as handling natural disasters. The <u>Internet</u> was created by the U.S. Department of Defense as an experiment.

A <u>Multinational Corporation</u> is a corporation that is involved in globalized manufacturing. Products can be made outside the U.S. with cheaper labor.

1.　　The internet created the ability for instant communication from anywhere in the world and access to information from worldwide resources.

2.　　In 1987, Russia and the U.S. agreed to eliminate many nuclear weapons in Europe. President Reagan challenged Mikhail Gorbachev to tear down the Berlin Wall and increase freedom in Eastern Europe. The fall of the Berlin Wall and the breakup of the U.S.S.R. ended the Cold War.

3.　　After September 11, 2001, Americans' sense of security was damaged. More than 3,000 Americans died in the attacks. The United States spent billions of dollars in the Middle East trying to find the terrorists behind these attacks. The government increased security at airports with each passenger being checked for weapons. The U.S. developed more aggressive actions against nations they believed supported terrorist groups.

*4.　　Advantages: More resources were available for other forms of international support, since money for weapons was not as necessary.
　　　　Disadvantages: The Cold War military was very large so as the military downsized, jobs had to be found for all these soldiers. The economy had grown because of producing weapons, so now this growth had to be replaced with other products.
　　　　New Challenges: There are new terror threats appearing every day. The problem is how to protect the American people and to fight the terrorists with a smaller military and with fewer weapons.

*5.　　Conservation –is the need to reduce air and water pollution in developing countries and for all countries to learn better methods to protect their natural environment.
　　　　Women at Work – This allows women everywhere to gain more freedom both politically and economically. Helping women to get the education necessary allows them to support their families and help economically.

Social Security – There are less people paying into Social Security, so when "baby boomers" (born in 1946-1964) are starting to collect, new financing must be found to pay for this government program.

Terrorism – Developing more support worldwide to fight terrorist groups such as Al Qaeda from attacking all over the world.

U.S. Foreign Policy – includes the stopping of terrorism around the world.

Immigration – The number of Latino and Asian immigrants have increased. We need to develop better methods for integrating these individuals into American society.

Crime – Internet crimes, and hate crimes are increasing. We need to develop better systems for rehabilitating criminals.

Education, Communication – We need to ensure that all Americans get an education regardless of economic position, and opportunities to continue their education after high school. We should ensure that global communication remains accessible to all but that privacy is protected.

Healthcare – Our national health care law states that everyone should have access to health insurance.

Poverty – We should decrease the level of poverty in the U.S. and help other nations to become more self-supporting.

Glossary

Word	Meaning
abolish (to)	to put an end to; do away with
abolition	the legal ending of slavery
abolitionist	one who wishes to do away with an evil, especially slavery
abridge (to)	to shorten by using fewer words but keeping the main contents
access (to)	to allow entry
according to	on the authority
accuse (to)	to formally charge with a wrongdoing
act	a law passed by the legislature
address	a formal speech
adopted	accepted; agreed to; taken as one's own
advocate	person who speaks or writes in support of something
affected	influenced, moved, persuaded
afford (to)	to be able to spend money on something
alliance	a close association for a common objective or mutual benefit
allotment	a share of something set aside for a specific purpose
ally	a country, person or group that are united for a common purpose
amendment	a change or an addition to a constitution or law
amnesty	a general pardon for a political offense against a government
amputate (to)	to cut off an arm or leg or other body part by surgery
ancestry	the people and culture from whom an individual descended from, ex: grandparents, great grandparents, etc.; forefathers
anthem	a song or hymn of praise or allegiance (national anthem)
appalled	shocked, dismayed
appointed	identified to take a job or office
arm (to)	to provide weapons to individuals
arrest (to)	to take into custody by the police
artillery	heavy weapons like cannons, machine guns, etc.

assassinate (to)	to kill (usually a politically important person) by a surprise attack
assault	sudden violent attack
assimilate (to)	to include a smaller culture into a larger group and remove all parts of the original culture
attorney	a person acting for another person at law; lawyer
authority	the power or right to give commands and make final decisions
autonomy	a self-governing state, community, or group
background	how a person lived, their social or cultural environment; a person's training, experience, or education
ban (to)	to not allow to have, to not use a thing or talk to a person
basin	a region drained by a river
bayonet	a knife-like blade on the shooting end of a rifle for man-to-man fighting
belongings	things a person owns
betray (to)	to give secret information to the enemy and lose the trust of one's country
bicentennial	200 years
bill	a suggested law proposed by a law maker
Bill of Rights	the first ten amendments to the constitution
blame (to)	to put the responsibility for an error (fault) on something or someone else
blazing desert	very hot desert
blitzkrieg	a sudden huge attack with combined air and ground forces to achieve a quick victory
blockade	any blocking action designed to cut off communication and trade for a nation
bombarded (to)	to attack with cannons or bombs
boom (to)	to grow or develop rapidly (like a business)
bootlegging	making, carrying or selling (usually liquor) illegally
boundary	the line, real or imaginary, that shows where a piece of land ends
boycott (to)	to join together to refuse to use, buy or sell something
brace	a piece of equipment used to support a weak part of the body

brash	hasty, reckless
break up a group (to)	to cause a large group to separate and leave individually
bribery	to give money to an official to gain a favor; illegal in the U.S.
brink	edge
brutal	cruel and unfeeling; violent or savage
bully	a person who hurts or frightens those who are smaller or weaker
Cabinet	a group of advisors to the president
campaign	series of military actions for a specific goal, or a series of planned actions for a specific purpose
candidate	a person who runs for office
capital	money in the form of savings that is invested in a business; the main city in a country where the government meets
Capitol	the building in which the U.S. Congress meets
carve (to)	to cut or shape carefully with a sharp knife or similar object
caste system	class system based upon birth, practiced in India in the past
catastrophe	any great or sudden disaster
cattle	farm animals like cows; livestock
cause	the thing a person fights for; reason
cease-fire	both sides agree to stop shooting weapons in a war
century	100 years
charity	the quality of being kind; an organization that gives to the less fortunate
check (to)	to control; to hold back; to restrain
choke (to)	to prevent from breathing by blocking the windpipe
chore	routine duty that is regularly done around the house or farm
citizen	a person having full rights in the place where he or she lives
civil	relating to private rights; having to do with government service
civilian	anyone who is not in the military service
claim (to)	to ask for as a right
clash (to)	to disagree strongly

clue	a piece of information leading to a solution to a problem
colonies	settlements in a new land
communism	a political system based on one-party government and state ownership of property; a classless society where there is an equal distribution of economic goods
compensation	payment for work done or for some other purpose
condemned (to)	to strongly disapprove
confederation	a loose alliance of political units (states) for a common purpose
confront (to)	to meet face to face
confrontation	defiant opposition meeting
Congress	the main law-making body of the United States
consequence	result
Constitution	the basic law of the United States
convention	a big meeting for some purpose
convict (to)	to find someone guilty of an offense or crime by a court of law
corner (to)	to trap with no possibility of escape
corrupt	to take bribes (money, gifts) to do something illegal or wrong
crash	to stop working/functioning
criminal	having to do with a wrongful act against society
crouch (to)	to bend low with your arms close to your body
crude	rough; not pure
crutch	a piece of equipment often used in pairs to help lame people to walk; typically, a staff with a hand grip and a padded cross piece on top that fits under the armpit
curse (to)	to use bad or improper words against someone or something
czar	the title of the leader of old Russia – a leader not chosen by the people
debate	a formal discussion of two opposing arguments
debt	something owed by one person to another or others

Declaration of Independence	public statement in which the Continental Congress in 1776 said that the 13 colonies were free from Great Britain
declare (to)	to make known openly
deficit spending	a government spending more money than it receives in revenue and taxes
dehydration	excessive loss of water from the body that can cause death
delegate	a person sent to speak or act for others; a representative
democracy	government of, by, and for the people
dependent	person needing support- a husband or wife, child, etc.
deprive	to take something away from a person using force
detonate (to)	to cause to explode with sudden violence
devastating	crushing, destructive; harmful
dictator	a ruler with absolute power and authority
disabled	unable to do what most people do physically or mentally; often unable to work
discourage (to)	to lose motivation
disgrace	a loss of honor, respect or reputation
disrupt (to)	to interrupt progress or cause confusion
distrustful	feeling or showing of doubt; unwilling to trust
domestic	having to do with our own country; relating to household or family
dominate (to)	to rule or control by superior power or influence a person
draft (to)	to choose or take a person for a specific purpose, usually used for military duty
drought	a long period of very low rainfall that limits plant growth
duck and cover (to)	to find shelter under something and then get low to the ground and cover one's head
dugout canoe	a boat made by hollowing out a big log
elected	chosen by the voters
eligible/eligibility	qualified for something; fit to be chosen
emulate(to)	to compete with equally and successfully by imitation
enforce (to)	to make people do something; to compel
entitled	qualified by right according to the law
evading (to)	to use cleverness or tricks to escape
evidence	data (statements, objects, etc.) that are used to establish truth or falsehood

exaggerate (to)	to overstate something to more than it is in reality
executive	the person who runs things; the boss; executive branch of government that enforces law
exotic	strange or different in an interesting or beautiful way; foreign
expedition	a journey for a specific purpose using special equipment, ships, people, etc.
export (to)	to send to foreign countries
extended	spread; reached out; made longer
famine	a shortage of food over a long period
fanatic	a person with strong beliefs whose actions go beyond what is reasonable
federal	form of government where power is divided between one central and several regional governments
fee	a charge for services or privileges; cost
feudalism	economic, social and political system in old Europe where serfs worked on the land and could not leave without the landowner's permission
fierce	violent, cruel wild behavior
figure out (to)	to estimate, determine, solve a problem
filthy	dirty
fine art	a major art form like painting, dance, music, sculpture, etc.
fledgling	a young, inexperienced country
flex	to tighten a muscle
floodgate	a gate for controlling a body of water; a control point for immigrants entering a country
folly	a foolish action
forage (to)	to search for food or supplies
former	the one before; the first
fortress	a place of exceptional security for defense
founded	started; built for the first time
fragile	delicate; easy to break
fugitive	a person who flees or tries to escape
furnace	an enclosed structure in which heat is produced
gadget	any small, mechanical device
gamble (to)	to take a risk to gain some advantage
gangster	person who is part of a gang, crew, group usually doing illegal actions

generosity/ generous	willingness to give or share; unselfishness
genocide	killing of a race of people, slaughter, massacre
globalization	the development of an increasing blended global economy
good	something you produce
graduate (to)	to complete a course of a study in a school or college
grant (to)	to give
greedy	desire for more than a person needs or deserves
grueling	requiring extreme effort
guarantee	a promise to do something; pledge; stand behind
hardship	trouble
harness power (to)	to control something to use for power
headed	led by
hemisphere	half of the world
hire (to)	to employ; give a job to
homesteader	a person who lives on a piece of land and develops it according to the Homestead Act of 1862
House of Representatives	the lower house of the U.S. Congress
immigrant	one who comes to a new country or region to settle there
imperial	having the position of emperor or king and controlling other countries or colonies
impress (to)	to make someone remember you; influence
inalienable	cannot be taken away or transferred
inconceivable	impossible to comprehend fully
infamous	having a bad reputation
infamy	disgrace, dishonor
inferior	lower in status or quality
informal	not according to rule; without ceremony; relaxed
insure (to)	to protect; make certain; guarantee
interfere (to)	to enter the affairs of others; to meddle; to clash
internment	to detain or hold in a special area within a country or definite area
interpret (to)	to help people to understand
invade (to)	to enter an area with the purpose of taking possession
isolationism	the belief that a country should not be involved in international agreements, etc.
issue	a problem needing a decision

jargon	specialized vocabulary for a profession or people in the same work
Jim Crow	phrase used to describe discrimination against and segregation of black people
judicial	having to do with courts and judges and interpreting the laws
junk	useless stuff
jury	a group of people who hear evidence in a case and make a decision
lasted (to)	to manage to continue
launch an attack (to)	to start an attack
lay off (to)	to be fired from a job
legacy	something that is passed down from previous generations
legend	story passed down for generations, believed to have basis in historical fact
legislative	having to do with making laws
legislature	the lawmaking body
levee	a raised ridge alongside a river constructed to prevent flooding
liberated (to)	to free from tyranny
loyal	true to one's friends or country
Magna Carta	an English document from 1215 that acted as a guarantee of basic rights for English barons
majority	the greater part, more than half of a total number
makeshift	a temporary substitute used in an emergency
malice	meanness, ill will
massacre (to)	to kill everyone that is present (men, women, children)
materialistic	to want wealth, comfort or pleasure more than other values
milestone	important event in history
militia	citizens who serve as soldiers rather than professional military
millennium	1000 years
mill	building with machinery for manufacturing or processing something
mine/miner	a large excavation of the earth to get minerals, like coal or gold
minimum	the smallest number or amount
minority	the lesser part, less than half of total number

misdemeanor	a minor offense that usually results is a fine, community service, or a small amount of jail time
misery	a condition of great suffering because of poverty or pain
moccasins	soft leather sandals/shoes worn by Native Americans
moral	having to do with right and wrong
mourn (to)	to feel sad
mow down (to)	to destroy or kill in great numbers in battle
mule	the animal that comes from mating a donkey and a horse
multinational	many nations
narrow	limited; not wide
national anthem	the official, national song of a country
nomadic (nomad)	wandering persons with no fixed home
novel	a long, fictional story
nutrient	part of food that is necessary to help one grow and develop
occupied (to)	to take possession of by force or by staying in the place, building, etc.
offense	a violation of the law or moral rule
offensive	insulting; causing anger or displeasure
oppressive	keeping people down by using cruel or unjust authority or power
ore	rock having some metal or mineral in it
organized crime	illegal acts done by criminals in organized groups or societies
outlaw	someone who breaks the law
outpost	any military base away from the main group
outskirts	on the borders of a city
overdose (to)	to take too large of an amount, usually medicine
override (to)	to vote again and a larger majority decides that the law should be approved; ex:: congress can override a presidential veto but 2/3rds must agree
overthrow (to)	to cause the downfall or destruction of a ruler by using force
overturn (to)	to reverse a law or decision by legal methods
pamphlet	a short collection of writings on a topic of current interest
parallel	latitude; imaginary horizontal lines that run from the equator north or south to the poles

paralyzed	a physical condition where something cannot move or is powerless
pardon (to)	to forgive
parliament	a government council, especially the national legislature of Great Britain
patriot	a person who loves and supports his or her own country
pay a fine (to)	to pay money to the court because you broke a minor law
peasant	in olden times-a class of small farmers or farm workers in Europe or Asia
peninsula	a piece of land surrounded on three sides by water
persecute (to)	to treat someone cruelly because of his or her beliefs
persecution	cruel treatment of a person because of his or her beliefs
petition	a formal written document addressed to a specific person/group that requests a specific action
Pilgrims	settlers who came from England and founded the colony of Plymouth in 1620
pit against (to)	to compete against someone
plantation	a farm or estate for growing certain crops, like cotton, tobacco, etc.
plateau	an elevated piece of land, tableland, mesa
plunder	valuables, holy items, goods taken illegally, usually in time of war
populous	full of people; crowded
posterity	future generations
pounded (to)	to attack with heavy gunfire until the target is flattened or destroyed
poverty	the state of being poor
preamble	the opening part of a statement
prejudice	a judgment or opinion formed before the facts are known
preserve (to)	to keep
presidency	the term during which a president is in office
privilege	a benefit or advantage
prohibited	not allowed or permitted; forbidden
prosecute (to)	to start a legal action against a person in a court of law
prosperity	condition of good fortune, success or wealth

proud	feeling satisfaction at one's achievements, possessions, connections, etc.
public office	a position in the service of a nation, state, or city
raid	a surprise attack by a small armed force
rain (weapons) (to)	to shower with objects
rascal	a dishonest and unreliable person
ratify (to)	to approve
raw material	material still in its natural condition before processing or manufacture
rebel	one who opposes government authority; name for a Confederate soldier
recession	temporary slowdown of business activity during a time that it usually is increasing
reckless	careless; not thinking about the consequences of an action
reconstruct (to)	to rebuild
recruit	the newest, least experienced soldier
redcoat	British soldier during the American Revolution
refuge	a place providing protection or shelter
regiment	military unit consisting of two or more battalions
register (to)	to have one's name written into a list of people who can take a job or can vote
reinforcements	strengthen with additional troops, ships, etc.
remarkable	unusual, extraordinary
remind (to)	to tell again
renovate (to)	to repair or remodel something to a good condition
rent (to)	to pay for the use of land, home, property; the money paid for such use
representative	a person chosen to act for another; delegate
republic	a system of representative government
resign from a job (to)	to choose to quit the job position
resource	any supply that will meet a need
retire (to)	to give up a job or office; to stop working
retreat (to)	to move back from the line of battle to a safe area: a private place of peace and security
revolutionaries	persons who participated in the American Revolution
right	something to which one has a just claim; any power or privilege given a person by law, custom, etc.
riveter	one who fastens plates or beams together with metal pins (rivets)

rubber mallet	a kind of hammer made from rubber with a large, heavy head and a short handle
rubble	broken pieces from a building because of earthquake or bombing
ruthless	hardhearted; cruel; without kindness
sacred	holy; having to do with religious respect
sacrifice (to)	to stop from having something in order to support a cause or ideal
savages	primitive people, usually cannot read or write
scandal	any act or person that shocks the moral feelings of a community and leads to disgrace
segregate (to)	to separate (often by force) one group of people from others, often based on race or ethnicity
self-educated	taught by oneself
Senate	the upper house of the U.S. Congress
serf(s)	a person in servitude, bound to the land and owned by the landowner
settle (to)	to set up a home; to live
settlement house	a community center offering social services for the poor
settler	a person who moves to a new colony and stays
shame (to)	to cause to feel that an action is unworthy, degrading, or dishonorable
shanty	a rough-built hut or shack
shelling	hitting something with cannonballs from a large gun
shield	type of weapon that is carried and used to cover a soldier so that a person's body is not hit
shortage	too small a number or amount; not enough
simmering	to remain just below the boiling point
sinew	tendon; a tough cord of tissue connecting muscle to bone
slam (to)	crash
slang	informal, nonstandard vocabulary
slaughter	the killing of people in large numbers usually in battle
slavery	the owning or keeping of slaves
slums	populated area of a city that has poor housing and lots of poverty
smear (to)	to harm someone's reputation by insults or slander
smuggle (to)	to secretly bring into or take out of a country illegally
sneak (to)	to move quietly and carefully to avoid being seen or heard

Social Security	a federal plan to take care of workers in their old age
span (to)	to extend across a space or opening; the distance between two supports of a bridge
sparked a war	an act that starts a conflict or war
spellbinding	holding attention as if in a magic spell; fascinated
spiritual song	black folk songs having a strong rhythm usually with a Biblical theme
squadron	a group of warships or planes, usually of the same type, assigned to a specific duty
stalemate	a point where neither side can gain an advantage; move or win
stampede	a sudden running away of a group of frightened animals
starvation	to suffer and die slowly from lack of food
station troops (to)	to position military forces in specific areas for a specific reason
stereotype	a monotonously predictable characterization of a person, without regard to individual differences
stifling	high heat where it is hard to breathe
stockpile (to)	to accumulate a large amount of something for future use
strategy/strategic	a careful plan or method for achieving a result
struggle (to)	to battle; fight; to make one's way with difficulty
strut	a type of walk where one tries to impress others or show off
subsidy	a government grant of money to private business for public benefit
subversive	trying to destroy an established government or institution
suggest (to)	to hint; mention
Sunday school	religious instruction on Sundays, usually by a church or temple
supreme	highest in importance
surge	a strong, sudden rush or increase
surrender (to)	to give up or quit trying
suspicious	feel mistrust, believe to be bad
swarmed (to)	to fill with a moving crowd or large group
swear (to)	to make a solemn promise under oath
sweeping law	comprehensive, extensive rule
system of checks and balances	a system in which each branch of government has powers that control the powers of others

tactics	the arranging and moving of military and naval forces for a short-term objective
temperance movement	the movement to get people to stop drinking alcoholic drinks
tend (to)	to take care of
tenements	apartments having minimum standards of safety and comfort
terms	parts or required action of an agreement
territory	land; region; land belonging to a government
ties	connections; have an even score
tinker (to)	to repair something in an unskilled or experimental way
topple (to)	to overthrow: replace using force (usually a government); to fall over
torpedo	self-propelled underwater weapon
totalitarianism	a form of government where the ruler is an absolute dictator
touch off (to)	to start as if by touching with fire
traitor	a person who works against his own country
trample (to)	to beat down or treat ruthlessly
tranquility	the condition of being calm, peaceful, or quiet
treason	betrayal of one's country
treasury	the country's money
treaty	agreement between nations
trenches	a deep cut in the ground (ditch) where troops would hide
tributary	flowing into a larger stream or lake
trigger an action (to)	to quick start an action
try (to)	to make an effort; to put an accused person on trial in court
tuition	money paid to a school in order to attend it
turn the tide (to)	to cause a complete reversal of a situation
tyranny	very cruel and unjust use of power and authority
unconstitutional	not according to the Constitution or law
uneducated	not trained; unskilled
uprising	rebellion; an outbreak against the government
uprooted (to)	to be forced to leave one's home and move to a new location
urban	relating to a city or town
veteran	a former member of the military

veto (to)	to refuse to allow a bill to become a law by not signing it
violate (to)	to break a law
wealth	riches; land; resources; money
well-off	prosperous; in fortunate living conditions
worship	to pray to; to pay honor and respect to

Bibliography

A Kid's Guide to America's Bill of Rights, Kathleen Krull, Avon Books, Inc., 1999.

American History, Know-the-Facts Review Game, Diana Abitz, Scholastic, Inc., 2005.

"American Authors" by Stuart Englert, AmericanProfile.com, March 2010.

Sacagawea: Heroine of the Lewis and Clark journey [Motion Picture]. United States: Questar, Inc. Forsberg, R. (Director). (2003).

A More Perfect Union, Betsy and Guilio Maestro, Mulberry Books, New York, 1987.

A Short History of the United States, Robert V. Remini, Harper Collins, 2008, pp245-336.

Barron's US Citizenship Test, Gladys E. Alesi, Barron's Educational Series, Inc., 2008.

Becoming a U.S. Citizen, Ilona Bray, NOLO, 2003, (chapter 6) pp 6/3-6/17.

Children Encyclopedia of American History, David C. King, DK Publishing, Inc. in association with the Smithsonian Institution, 2003.

Encyclopedia of Native American Tribes: Third Edition, C. Waldman, Checkmark Books, New York, NY, 2006.

How the U.S. Government Works, Syl Sobel, Barron's Educational Series, Inc., 1999.

If you were there when They Signed the Constitution, Elizabeth Levy, Scholastic, Inc., 1987.

Pass the U.S. Citizenship Test, 3rd edition, Learning Express, 2008, multiple pages.

Shh! We're Writing the Constitution, Jean Fritz, G.P. Putnam's Sons, 1987.

The U.S. Constitution and You, Syl Sobel, Barron's Educational Series, Inc., 2001.

The Trail of Tears: Cherokee Legacy [Documentary]. United States: Rich-Heape Films, Inc. Richie, C. (Director). (2006).

U.S. Citizenship Test, 7th edition, Gladys Alesi, Barron's Educational Series, 2008, multiple pages.

What Every 1-6 Grader Needs to Know series, E.D. Hirsch, Jr., Doubleday, 1991, American history sections.

What's Government? Nancy Harris, Heinemann Library, Chicago, Illinois, 2008.

http://www.nytimes.com/2012/04/03/science/civil-war-toll-up-by-20-percent-in-new-estimate.html

Acknowledgments

This book could not have been completed without the help from the many different individuals who supported me throughout this project. Many of my students and colleagues read various sections and provided valuable critiques to improve the material. The editorial support from Char Luttrell and Susan Oppat helped me to fine-tune this topic and ensure that it remained readable for my audience. Kathy Berliner was invaluable with typing support, research, and suggestions. Craig Tollenaar creatively translated my words into the illustrations that I used in the book. And, without my very supportive husband, Bill who capably fact checked every version, this book would not be possible.

Index